Pathways to Learning
in Rett Syndrome

Jackie Lewis and Debbie Wilson

David Fulton Publishers

David Fulton Publishers
2 Park Square, Milton Park, Abingdon, Oxon OX14 4RN

270 Madison Avenue, New York, NY 10016

First published in Great Britain by David Fulton Publishers 1998
Reprinted 2001, 2003
Transferred to digital printing

David Fulton Publishers is an imprint of the Taylor & Francis Group, an informa business

British Library Cataloguing in Publication Data
A catalogue record for this book is available from the British Library

ISBN 1–85346–533–X

Typeset by Textype Typesetters, Cambridge

Contents

Foreword: Yvonne Milne, Founder and President UKRSA   v

Acknowledgements   vii

Introduction: The girl with Rett Syndrome   1

Part 1: Factors Affecting Learning   **9**

1   Physical Factors   10

2   Social Factors   16

3   Emotional Factors   23

4   Intellectual Factors   32

Part 2: The Specific Barriers to Learning in Rett Syndrome   **41**

5   Hand Dysfunction   42

6   Delayed Response   49

7   Apraxia   53

Part 3: Implications for Teachers   **57**

8   Attitudes and Values   59

9   The Curriculum   80

10   Specific Teaching Strategies   110

Bibliography   125

Index   131

Foreword

In 1985, when the work of the newly formed United Kingdom Rett Syndrome Association began in earnest, knowledge about the best possible care, education and treatment for RS girls and women was in its infancy. Parents, carers and all involved in any way with these people were thirsty for information which could enable them to understand better their social, emotional, physical and intellectual needs. It was obvious from the outset that all those affected had severe and complex learning difficulties, combined with physical difficulties, yet their bright eyes, knowing looks and their distinct personalities gave clues to their true potential to thrive, to learn and to develop, in spite of all this.

How to realise this potential to the full has been the greatest challenge to all those close to the Rett person in the intervening years. During this time interest in this puzzling syndrome has gathered momentum. Professionals from all disciplines, the families and the Rett Syndrome sufferers themselves have consistently added to the growing pool of knowledge that is so vitally needed.

This study by Jackie Lewis and Debbie Wilson, so aptly entitled 'Pathways to Learning in Rett Syndrome' represents a very important and valuable contribution to this fund of knowledge as it helps to unravel the mysteries surrounding the education of the RS sufferer, to give us a greater understanding of her needs and a clearer insight into her world. After many years of observation and research, both as teachers and, in Jackie's case as a mother involved in day-to-day living with a Rett sufferer, they give the clear message that there are ways to penetrate what at first sight may appear to be insurmountable barriers to learning; and that all the strategies used are still relevant after education in school is complete.

These well documented strategies for the Rett girl or woman will be of help throughout her life and will serve as important sources of reference for all who are involved in her care.

Yvonne Milne
Founder and President, UK Rett Syndrome Association

Acknowledgements

We would like to acknowledge the help and guidance given to us by teachers and parents of the girls with Rett Syndrome. The United Kingdom Rett Syndrome Association and the International Rett Syndrome Association have been of invaluable assistance. We would especially like to recognise the support given by Kathy Hunter in assisting us in our research in America and Canada.

We would also like to thank Yvonne Milne, Hilary Cass and Una Chester for their invaluable editorial advice.

Introduction: The girl with Rett Syndrome

Rett Syndrome is a complex and challenging disability, so far only diagnosed in girls. Apparently normal at birth, those affected suffer a dramatic regression of development, resulting in profound and multiple learning difficulties and physical disabilities.

Although first identified in 1966, by Dr Andreas Rett, the condition went largely unnoticed until 1983. Since then, medical research has been carried out world-wide (Van Acker 1991). Dr Alison Kerr, who is at the forefront of medical research and treatment of girls with Rett Syndrome in the UK, suggested that it affected more than 1 in 10,000 live female births (Kerr 1994). The cause is currently thought to be an unpredicted development of a fault in a gene in the X chromosome.

The girl usually reaches broadly typical milestones of development for about the first year of life, until reaching a sudden stop. A period of regression follows, during which she appears to lose many of her previously acquired skills. Research has suggested that, although each girl will have made early progress within the accepted range, she will have been affected well before the regression period (Nomura *et al.* 1987; Moeschler 1988; Kerr 1994). After this period of regression, which may last for a few days or many months:

- profound learning difficulties are evident which will remain throughout her life. These are such that she will always be totally dependent on others for all aspects of her care;
- stereotypical hand movements develop, such as hand clapping, patting or wringing;
- physical difficulties may emerge, some of which will become evident as she grows. Some girls may walk – albeit with a wide, broad-based gait, some girls may never walk. Some may develop scoliosis, and some suffer from epilepsy.

1

However, 'many reach adult life in robust health' (Kerr 1994).

This tragic, puzzling disorder is characterised by attractive girls with, often, alert expressions apparently registering events – although their responses may be delayed or non-existent. Although all those who are diagnosed with Rett Syndrome follow a broadly similar developmental path, there is an enormous variation in the degree to which they are affected.

Medical research has resulted in a strong affiliation to 'therapies' (physiotherapy, hydrotherapy, music therapy, aromatherapy etc.) in planning to meet the girls' needs, and there is no doubt that these are of vital importance. It is not intended within this publication to focus on the therapeutic aspects of meeting these pupils' needs, which are well documented elsewhere by specialists in those fields.

There has, however, been little research undertaken into the range of skills individuals affected by Rett Syndrome may demonstrate, the ways in which their learning may be promoted, and the implications of this diagnosis for teachers.

As Rett Syndrome is a newly described disorder, and because of the lack of applied educational research, very little has been written about appropriate educational programming for girls with Rett Syndrome. Due to its relative rarity until now, most schools have not had a number of girls on whom to provide programming and planning.

(Hunter in IRSA 1990, p.1)

The research project

In 1991, the United Kingdom Rett Syndrome Association (UKRSA, now know as RSAUK) was a rapidly growing organisation, having contact with approximately 350 girls through their parents and carers. Established in 1985 by Yvonne Milne, a parent of a girl with Rett Syndrome, the association offered support to parents and carers through a quarterly newsletter, an annual conference and a network of parent-to-parent assistance. Included in the membership was a growing body of professionals involved with those affected by this newly diagnosed condition – doctors, therapists and teachers.

There was, therefore, an established forum where issues of concern to all those involved in the care of girls with Rett Syndrome could be aired.

The committee of the UKRSA were able to identify members' queries, and address issues through their annual conference programme or publications in the newsletter.

One such issue was the lack of applied educational research. As knowledge regarding medical research grew, the girls' medical needs became increasingly well-known and met. Their educational needs, however, remained an unknown quantity. The UKRSA received an increasing number of queries regarding the specific special educational needs of those diagnosed with Rett Syndrome, but those needs were not, at that time, known or understood.

The researchers

One of the researchers was a member of the UKRSA Executive Committee during the time that questions were being raised by parents and professionals about the education of girls with Rett Syndrome. This researcher, a parent of an affected girl, discussed this lack of applied research with her daughter's teacher, and from these discussions the research project was planned.

The two researchers had already undertaken work together in this area, through published articles and conference addresses. A collaborative research project was, thus, undertaken in which each partner brought complementary expertise – one as a parent and the other as a teacher, but both with some experience of the condition.

The aim of the research project

The aim of the research initially was to collate existing practice and to disseminate information regarding the meeting of the special educational needs of girls with Rett Syndrome. This would embrace the educational settings, the staffing, the curriculum and specific strategies used by teachers. Any particular challenges faced by teachers would also be sought, in order to identify specific difficulties and seek strategies which might help to overcome them.

Rett Syndrome had only been recognised in this country since 1983. Prior to this, the girls were likely to have been categorised more generally within a 'special care' class. It was likely, then, that appropriate educational provision for girls with Rett Syndrome would be similarly applicable to other pupils with a profound and multiple learning difficulty.

The lack of earlier research into the educational needs of girls with Rett Syndrome resulted in very little information on which to form the basis of the research.

The pilot study

The purpose of the pilot study was to undertake a survey of the current ways in which the educational needs of girls with Rett Syndrome were being met. The study aimed to discover and explore the nature of the educational provision being offered to pupils with Rett Syndrome, to identify common difficulties, and to share teachers' knowledge and experience in effectively meeting their needs.

The survey population

The survey population consisted of 28 class teachers, and related to 42 girls with Rett Syndrome, aged from 5 to 19 years, educated in 26 schools in the UK, the USA and Canada. The survey population was selected by the following methods:

- Through the UKRSA volunteers were sought who felt they had something interesting to share.
- Cluster sampling, where schools were known to have several girls with Rett syndrome or where there were several schools catering for this syndrome in a close area;
- Schools where a particular strategy was known or thought to be being explored, or where a girl had an atypical skill within the syndrome.
- Sample groups were suggested by the UKRSA's sister association, the International Rett Syndrome Association, regarding schools in the United States and Canada.

Resources available

Detailed plans, outlining the aims of the research and the financial implications, were drawn up and applications made to Charitable Trusts. Funding was obtained from three bodies.

The collecting and collating of data

The collecting and collating of research data was an important element of the research. The very small number of pupils affected by Rett Syndrome, and their widespread locations, meant that no one teacher was likely to have met more than a few girls. In order to build up a broad picture of the characteristics and educational implications of Rett Syndrome, visits were planned to schools. Informal, unstructured participant observation in classrooms offered opportunities to undertake first hand data collection. Observations were recorded in note form, and video and photographs were used when permitted.

Teachers' knowledge and experience was sought through semi-structured interviews, in which a questionnaire formed the basis of discussion. This questionnaire sought information on the type of school, number of staff and additional provision for each subject, the girls' timetable, curriculum and teaching priorities. In addition, data was collected regarding activities, equipment or approaches which teachers had felt were effective, any particular challenges faced by the staff and an opportunity for teachers to pass on any other information.

Data gathered was entered into a database, and the results analysed.

Further studies

Communication in girls with Rett Syndrome

One area of concern highlighted within the pilot study was that of communication in girls with Rett Syndrome. No specific research or formal assessment had been undertaken into the communication skills of girls with Rett Syndrome, so a further, small-scale, study was planned.

The aim of the communication study would be to examine the methods of communication most commonly used by the girls, and to explore strategies to assess and develop them. A new sample of 12 pupils with Rett Syndrome were selected, and although parts of this study did not result in useful data, it led to a further study with 16 girls using Kiernan Reid's Pre-Verbal Communication Schedule.

Parental evaluation of the education offered to girls with Rett Syndrome

The pilot study also highlighted the issues surrounding home and school working together. A further small-scale study was planned which aimed to identify and examine attitudes held by parents and to identify factors which they thought valuable in the education of their daughter. This was achieved by means of an anonymous questionnaire from which data was categorised and examined.

A summary of the research findings is illustrated in the model opposite entitled 'Pathways through the barriers to learning in Rett Syndrome'. The following chapters outline in more detail the results which led to compilation of this model, and possible strategies (or pathways) which were suggested during the research.

Pathways through the barriers to learning in Rett Syndrome

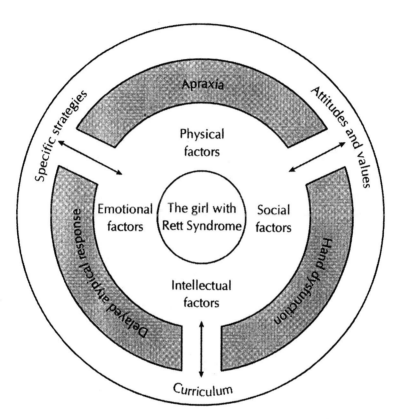

Debbie Wilson and Jackie Lewis
UKRSA 1993
Modified 1997

Part 1

Factors Affecting Learning

In the UK, the 1970 Education Act established the rights of pupils with severe and complex learning difficulties to enter the education system. Prior to this, such children had been deemed 'ineducable'. The Warnock Report (DES 1978) further developed the position of this group of pupils by stating that the goals of education were the same for all pupils:

> whereas for some (children) the road they have to travel towards the goal is smooth and easy, for others it is fraught with obstacles . . . nevertheless, for them too, progress will be possible and their educational needs fulfilled as they gradually overcome one obstacle after another.

Meeting the educational needs of girls with Rett Syndrome can only be effective within the context of meeting their needs as people. Each of them will have her own personal needs in addition to her educational requirements. These needs may be varied and complex, and best met by a variety of professionals. Teachers, therefore, will need to tap into the expertise of parents and other professionals in order to plan an holistic approach to educating the girl with Rett Syndrome.

The girls' needs as people are no different to our own. We all need to be fed, to be warm, to remain as healthy as possible, to be loved and to have opportunities to influence our own lives for the better. It is, therefore, necessary to ensure that these basic factors affecting individuals' lives are addressed satisfactorily before effective teaching and learning can commence.

Chapter 1

Physical Factors

There are a variety of physical factors which may affect any girl with Rett Syndrome to differing degrees, the most common of which are as follows:

Physical disabilities

Many pupils with Rett Syndrome have quite severe physical disabilities. Some remain non-ambulant, whilst others learn to walk – sometimes at a much later age than is typical. Of those who do learn to walk, many do so with a characteristic broad-based and stiff gait. Lindberg (1991) described girls who rocked, bent their bodies, staggered or showed problems with balance. Few in this study developed response reactions to protect themselves; for example, when falling few girls were able to use their hands to save themselves. A large number of them are nervous when walking on uneven surfaces.

Many girls have poor balance and difficulty in controlling their position and movements. Some may dislike intensely being handled – when being dressed or doing physiotherapy, for example.

It is also not unusual for a girl with Rett Syndrome to have great difficulty in grading her movements or carrying out transitional movements, causing problems in moving from sitting to standing or vice versa, or lifting her foot onto a step.

A fairly common condition, for some, as they grow up, is that of scoliosis (a sideways bending of the spine). Physiotherapy, hydrotherapy and regular clinical reviews are therefore necessary to help prevent, delay or monitor such possible changes to the physical health of the girl.

Epilepsy is thought to be common in around 55 per cent of the girls (UKRSA database).

Sensory perception difficulties

Girls with Rett Syndrome often appear to have difficulty in moderating their sensory reactions. A quiet sound may be perceived by them as very loud, or a strong pain not apparently felt at all. Lindberg (1991) referred to 'a sensory and perceptual chaos' which may overwhelm and confuse them. The child with Rett Syndrome then, may appear hypersensitive to everything or, conversely, show an apparent indifference to the outside world. She may over-react to what is, to us, a normal range of sights and sounds, or she may 'shut down' in order to cope.

Females with Rett Syndrome are often described as having a high pain threshold. Lindberg suggested that they may feel internal pain (e.g. stomach ache) more acutely than external pain (e.g. an injection). They may also experience problems in expressing any pain which they do feel, and any such reaction may be significantly delayed.

Vision

Many girls, although not suffering from recognised visual problems, use their sight in an unusual way. Particularly when in an unfamiliar setting, girls may only use their peripheral vision (looking out of the corner of their eyes) or use fleeting glances. In more familiar settings, or with people they know well, their gaze can be very strong indeed.

Hearing

As stated earlier, girls may have difficulty in coping in very noisy settings. Many of them have clear preferences for particular types of music – quite what type will vary according to taste! It appears that they can recognise and interpret familiar sounds and react accordingly.

There are also other physical disabilities inherent in Rett Syndrome which are:

- A delayed or atypical response
- Apraxia
- Hand dysfunction

(Lewis and Wilson 1991)

11

Arguably, these three disabilities create the most challenging aspects of teaching girls with Rett Syndrome, and are always present in every case, to varying degrees. These three specific 'barriers to learning' will be dealt with in greater detail further on.

Therapeutic intervention

Currently, there is no cure for Rett Syndrome, and one can only treat the particular symptoms.

> Physiotherapists and occupational therapists have a crucial role to play in maintaining or improving functional movement, mobility, preventing deformities and keeping the girls in contingent contact with their environments.

> (Van Acker 1991)

Although there are many similarities in the Rett Syndrome diagnosis, responses to treatment will vary enormously. Many girls may become very fearful during therapy, when they have not initiated movements for themselves.

Spasticity is a fairly common problem, and it is thought that it is this which may be responsible for breathing/swallowing problems (Hanks 1986 in Van Acker 1991) and – at least in part – the high incidence of scoliosis in girls with Rett Syndrome.

The ability to walk remains the most important skill to develop and maintain. Some may never have learned this skill, others may lose it after regression. Attempts to develop independent standing and walking must be given a high priority. Unfortunately, many of the commonest walking aids, such as rollators, will be of limited use due to the absence of purposeful hand function.

Many girls will require Piedro boots, inserts and the like – combined with properly fitted wheelchairs and seating in order to maintain physical skills.

Stereotypical hand movements are one of the most distinctive features of Rett Syndrome, and it is these which result in the lack of purposeful hand use. These movements evolve with age, from simple, rapid movements. Gradually they become slower and more complex before ultimately becoming slow and less complicated. The hand movements will increase when the girl is under stress and usually cease completely during sleep.

Attempts to modify these hand movements through behaviour modification, medication or the use of splints have proved unsuccessful so far. Indeed, many people with Rett Syndrome are unable to tolerate splints at all, and will become very distressed.

Many girls with Rett Syndrome have a marked tendency to lose weight and they may require a high calorie diet. Since this may be combined with difficulties in chewing/swallowing, more specialised advice may be required. Constipation may be a problem with some, often due to a failure to drink enough fluids or eat enough fibre. Dietary measures, sometimes combined with laxatives or the like, may be necessary.

Findings from observations and questionnaires

A number of teachers highlighted coping with the physical disabilities in Rett Syndrome as challenging in their teaching. Despite this, less than half the girls saw a physiotherapist once a week or more – although many teachers could approach their therapist for advice if they felt the need. Only 8 of the 42 saw an occupational therapist regularly.

Rhythmic intention

This was suggested as helpful in meeting some of the physical needs of girls with Rett Syndrome. Rhythmic intention is one of the 'facilitators' of conductive education. It is described as having two important factors; firstly to make activity voluntary, and secondly to provide rhythm. Counting or singing can be used, on the pupils' behalf, if they are unable to participate. Thus, 'I raise my right arm' (verbal intention). '1,2,3,4,5' (rhythm). Longhorn (1988) noted that parents of pupils with profound and multiple learning difficulties frequently used particular songs with particular actions, and lots of repetition, which they felt had 'improved their limited memories' (p.173).

The principles of rhythmic intention, in which actions are practised within a repetitive routine with clear cues and signals, would appear to offer a way forward for some girls with Rett Syndrome in relation to their

13

profound learning difficulties, apraxia and delayed response, and this would benefit from further study.

Hydrotherapy

Hydrotherapy is the performance of physiotherapy exercises in warm water, combined with therapeutic and recreational aspects. It has been suggested that the stress, fear, anxiety and muscle spasm which create tension may be alleviated through the relaxation gained whilst exercising in water. It would seem to offer some girls with Rett Syndrome the opportunity to make movements which are otherwise difficult, and offer useful leisure and recreational curriculum opportunities which could extend beyond school.

Medical research institute

During the observations, there was an opportunity to meet with a team of professionals undertaking medical research into Rett Syndrome. Although these were only small scale projects, a brief description may serve to contribute further to the knowledge and understanding of the physical aspects of Rett Syndrome.

Sleep programmes used with girls with Rett Syndrome
Results from this research, comparing 20 girls with Rett Syndrome with 20 other children, suggested that the girls had 19 per cent less night time sleep than the control group, and 25 per cent more daytime sleep. It was suggested that daytime sleep was inappropriate as the girls got older, affecting their ability to concentrate and putting a severe strain on the carers. Four girls with Rett Syndrome, aged 3, 4, 13 and 19 had undertaken a behavioural programme to reduce night-time awakenings, and all of them had improved.

Eating programmes used with girls with Rett Syndrome
This had been undertaken with three girls, at least one of whom had no self-feeding skills prior to the programme. If any girl had problems with chewing or swallowing, she was first referred to an occupational therapist.

Backward chaining techniques, combined with prompting, operated for the first 20 mouthfuls – when the girls were hungriest, the food looks and smells its best and the motivation is highest.

Breath-holding in girls with Rett Syndrome

All girls with Rett Syndrome can have episodes of breath-holding, and these may increase as they get older. We all breathe in oxygen and breathe out carbon dioxide. It is the percentage of each which determines breathing. When a girl hyperventilates, the level of carbon dioxide drops, so there is no reason to breathe in. The girl stops breathing, so the carbon dioxide builds up again which is her stimulus to resume breathing.

Most breathing problems increase during sleep, but in girls with Rett Syndrome this is not the case – the girls do not hold their breath at all during sleep. The conclusion, therefore, is that the reason for breath-holding is a behavioural one but, importantly, not a conscious choice. In girls with Rett Syndrome, breath-holding is a compulsive habit and they cannot stop themselves from doing it.

It was felt that episodes of breath-holding may increase when a girl is bored or upset, and could possibly be improved by distracting or amusing her.

The degree of physical disability with which girls with Rett Syndrome are left with will vary enormously. Maintenance of physical health, rather than improved skills, may well be the primary goal for many girls. Strategies to facilitate physical well-being are outlined in the final chapter.

Chapter 2

Social Factors

'Social development – socialisation – is the process of learning the skills and attitudes which enable the individual to live easily with other members of their community.' Minett (1994)

Humans are social beings, instinctively needing others to one degree or another. From the earliest days company comforts the crying baby. A lack of company leads to loneliness which leads to unhappiness.

Children who are happy value themselves and have self-respect. They have a positive image of themselves, which enables them to become more self-confident and self-reliant. They have self-esteem, which gives them self-confidence and self-reliance. Self-confidence enables all children to realise that they can cope with the people they meet and the usual situations in which they find themselves. They come to trust their own judgement, become more self-reliant when they are allowed to choose.

Disability is recognised as an important factor that can severely affect self-esteem, and, for the girl with Rett Syndrome, maintaining a positive self-image is an important challenge facing all who work with her.

It is recognised that self-esteem will be developed when children receive praise for what they can do rather than criticism for what they can't. When pupils receive encouragement they are more likely to develop new skills. Due to her severe disabilities the girl with Rett Syndrome is completely dependent on others to assist her in acquiring new skills, and encouragement will need to be constant, staff seeking opportunities to praise and encourage her forward.

In order to avoid her becoming a completely passive person, opportunities will need to be sought in which the pupil may exercise choice, allowing her some control. If she is allowed to show her feelings in whatever way she can, and these are acknowledged, her self-esteem will be helped.

Social development and Rett Syndrome

Girls with Rett Syndrome are described as being very sociable, enjoying the company of others immensely. Newsletters of both the United Kingdom Rett Syndrome Association and the International Rett Syndrome Association, (based in the United States) provide ample evidence of this in the many articles written by their parents and friends describing their participation in, and enjoyment of, a wide variety of social activities both within the family and in the wider community.

Allan (1991) describes the girl with Rett Syndrome as having 'willing sociability'. The girl may be willing, but her disabilities prevent her being able to form relationships alone, and each situation will need setting up for her. Recognition of familiar faces is often evident, though this may take a long time to build up. Time will be needed for her to get to know her friends, and they will need to be aware that they will have to build their relationship gently and carefully.

Those who know girls with Rett Syndrome well report that they frequently initiate or conclude social contact. Parents report instances where their daughter actively looks away from certain people, or closes her eyes when they talk to her. She may seek out with her eyes a favoured person in a large gathering, gazing intently at them until they respond.

It has been noted that those with Rett Syndrome enjoy the company of their peers (Lindberg 1991). They enjoy mixing with disabled and non-disabled people, and, although they may be only able to sit and watch, or to participate only with adult support, their great pleasure is immediately apparent to the observer.

It is also suggested that they need to meet others with the same condition. When two girls with Rett Syndrome were observed, Lindberg describes a 'very close and special contact' between them. This consisted of them seeking each other out in the room, moving close together, glancing at each other and intensifying their hand movements while smiling to themselves.

The people surrounding someone affected by Rett Syndrome guide the development of her social well-being.

At home

The primary and most important social contact will occur in her home and be, usually, largely dependent on her parents or carers. Her family, both immediate and extended, may form the major part of her world for many years – considerably longer than with other children because of her great difficulties. Because opportunities for social interaction will always need to be created for her, the family usually have this responsibility long term. This will contrast with her brothers and sisters, who, as they grow older, form their own friendships away from the family.

How her close carers view her disability, how they cope with it in social situations and how she is encouraged to cope, will affect her self esteem. How do carers cope with people who stare? Is it possible to gauge how the girl feels being constantly stared at when out? How does it feel to be cooed-over at 16? How does it feel to always attract pitying glances from strangers?

At school

Students with Rett Syndrome of school age in the UK were found to be most often educated in maintained special schools for children with severe learning difficulties. (Lewis and Wilson 1991). This is also true in the United States (Holmes *et al.* in IRSA 1990). However, special schools differ greatly in their structure and population. The private sector of education was also found to offer a variety of educational settings that were considered appropriate.

One clear exception described was where pupils with Rett Syndrome, and other profoundly disabling conditions, were educated in mainstream schools along with their peer group. This is an issue about which there has been much discussion in recent years; however this is not the place in which to enter into it, save to say that there is much literature on the subject. Relevant examples of such integration were described by Jupp (1992), who outlined integration work in the North of England; and by Perkovich, (in IRSA 1990) who described similar work with a 12 year old student with Rett Syndrome in Toronto.

Parents have had a large part to play in the decision as to the appropriate educational setting for their children. In the UK the girls' 'statement of

Special Educational Needs' includes a contribution by the parents, and the importance of parental contribution was enshrined in both the 1981 and 1990 Education Acts, both of which promoted the idea of 'Parents as Partners'. This was further developed in the Code of Practice on the identification and assessment of special educational needs (DFE 1994).

Findings from observations and questionnaires

The schools

Schools visited in the study catered for children with a wide variety of needs. Most were special schools – some catering for children with a wide range of learning difficulties, and some more specialised. Some girls were also visited whose education took place in mainstream school.

Using the model of classification of school setting outlined by Holmes *et al.* in IRSA 1990 , it is possible to picture all school settings as part of a continuum from 'most-restrictive' to 'least-restrictive', where the most restrictive is a residential hospital, and the least an integrated classroom in a mainstream school. In between are many possible settings – special day schools, part-time special class with support in classroom among others. Girls with Rett Syndrome were observed receiving their education at many points along this continuum, though the largest number were found towards the 'most restrictive' end.

There were a number of pupils visited who were educated in privately-run residential schools, although most were in state-funded day schools. Those in residential schools tended to be the older girls of 12 and over.

The staff

Most students with Rett Syndrome, with the exception of those in mainstream school, were educated in classes where the teacher / pupil ratio was between 1:4 and 1:9. All classes visited also had classroom assistants. The nature of the assistance varied greatly. A few teachers received qualified assistance from up to three Nursery Nurses, whilst others received unqualified assistance only, one teacher visited having six unqualified assistants working in the class.

A few girls visited received one-to-one support in class. This appeared to be for a variety of reasons and depended on their perceived needs within their setting.

Grouping

Pupils with Rett Syndrome were observed being educated in classes with other children of the same or similar age. In a special school this is not as clear-cut as in mainstream, where classes are generally arranged in year cohorts. In special education, grouping was often found to be based on the needs of the children as well as age. Thus, special school classes sometimes contained a range of ages, usually within two or three years and sometimes far more It was expressed by teachers that it was desirable that these pupils be educated along with their peers, since it allowed age-appropriate adaptation of the individual's curriculum

Classes for pupils with severe learning difficulties

The greatest number of students with Rett Syndrome that were observed were in classes along with children with a wide range of severe learning difficulties. It was reported on several occasions that they enjoyed the company of other more active and 'busy' children. However, the vulnerability of the girl with Rett Syndrome, her lack of awareness of danger and inability to request assistance, naturally caused parents and teachers considerable anxiety.

As with all children, as she progressed through her years in education, changes of class and school sometimes occurred, and this was reported as a time of anxiety both for the girl herself and for her parents. The difficulties experienced at times of change were highlighted by one teacher who saw as a priority in her teaching that her pupil 'accept new situations without displaying aggressive behaviour.' All staff will need to be aware that for these students and their parents, times of change will require sensitive and careful preparation and handling.

Throughout her schooling the group that she is placed with will need careful introduction to both her and her parents. Many children with severe learning difficulties can exhibit unpredictable behaviour to which the girl with Rett Syndrome would be vulnerable. Staff will need to be aware of, and deal sensitively with, the understandable concerns that may arise.

The girl with Rett Syndrome will always be totally dependent on those around her. With the very large majority of children, including many of those in special schools, a growing level of independence is expected as the child grows older. This will not always be true of the girl with Rett Syndrome and parental concerns are likely to continue throughout her education.

20

Specialist classes for pupils with profound and multiple learning difficulties

A proportion of the girls visited were found in small units or classes within special schools along with a small number of other pupils who experience profound and multiple learning difficulties. Their classmates were usually non-ambulant, often being more profoundly disabled than the girl with Rett Syndrome, and there was a heavy emphasis on the therapeutic and sensory aspects of their education. It was reported that these girls benefited from the quiet, calm atmosphere of such classrooms.

Residential schools

Visits were made to two residential schools, where the student lived at school for all or part of her education. At one such school, six students with Rett Syndrome had been identified within a peer group, and constituted their own class as part of a residential educational programme. It was observed that these students, all aged between 13 and 19, interacted with each other – touching, laughing and looking. An extract from observational notes provides the following example:

C is sitting next to H.

H has her kitchen timer on the table to remind her about her toilet programme.

Both have their boxes, (current work) on the table in front of them.

C slowly knocks the kitchen timer a little.

H giggles as it moves, watching the clock, watching her friend . . .

It was clear that although similar in many ways, the students displayed widely differing personalities and abilities. The quiet, calm pace seemed to be of benefit to the students and typical behaviours such as hand-wringing and hyperventilation appeared considerably reduced.

Mainstream schools

The teachers concerned with those girls placed in mainstream schools reported that they were very popular among the other pupils in the classes. One teacher said of a girl at middle school 'She independently approaches staff and peers and engages them in eye contact. She has a core group of six to eight friends with whom she spends time on the playground and in the cafeteria.'

The same teacher also reported out of school contact with her school friends such as going out to tea with them. Another girl, in a reception class, was also described as being very popular. In this case, one or two children played closely with her and nearly all in the class were described as being 'very friendly and interested in her'.

In some high schools positive attempts to encourage sociability were in place. Under the 'Buddy' system, students were able to obtain merits towards an accredited qualification for assisting their peers with special needs. Examples were described of typical students suggesting age-appropriate ideas as to how to adapt the curriculum to meet individual special needs, or arranging to take a friend with special needs out for an evening's bowling.

The main finding about social development was that, wherever they were being educated, girls with Rett Syndrome were popular with their teachers and classmates. It appeared that somehow, despite their very grave difficulties, their personalities shone through.

Strategies to promote social well-being are outlined in the final chapter.

Chapter 3

Emotional Factors

Emotions are feelings such as fear, excitement, love, happiness, worry, sorrow, anger, contentment, frustration, and a great many more. Young children often show their feelings clearly, learning to control their feelings as they develop emotionally. Emotional development is influenced by the inborn temperament, the environment and the state of health of the child (Minett 1994). Temperament is entirely dependent on the inherited genes. Some people are naturally shy and others more outgoing; some worry while others appear carefree.

The home environment in which a child grows up will affect emotional development. The behaviour of the people in the home; the conditions that exist there; the effects of the fortunes and misfortunes of life; all have their part to play in developing each child's way of expressing feelings. The type of training the child receives from the adults around and the examples seen again and again will affect the way in which feelings become controlled.

Health and emotions

There is a strong link between a child's state of health and feelings (Minett 1994). In the case of short-term illness, it is easy to see that when a usually healthy child feels unwell she will be unhappy, confused and worried at the strangeness of the illness. Long-term illness presents a slightly different picture:

> Long term illness or handicap can have a marked effect on a child's emotional development. What sort of effect it will have depends on the child's inborn temperament and the care and training she receives.
>
> (Minett 1994)

Stress

All children react emotionally to stress in their lives. There are certain events which can be identified as major causes of stress, which include:

- a new baby in the immediate family;
- the death of a relative or pet;
- the break up of the family;
- separation from a parent;
- starting school or playgroup;
- moving home;
- abuse.

(Minett 1994)

Being profoundly disabled does not exempt children and young people from suffering stress. In the case of Rett Syndrome it can happen that they are experiencing stress but are unable to communicate their feelings. Everyone working with the student needs to be constantly vigilant for individual signs of stress.

Adolescence

Adolescence can be an emotional time for all young people. The stress brought about by the physical and hormonal changes taking place is often held responsible for the notorious mood swings of adolescents.

> At a biological level adolescence is very eventful and it would be strange if all the changes which take place over a relatively short period of time should pass by without any emotional effects on young people and their parents.

(Petrie 1990)

The girl with Rett Syndrome, along with all her peers, has to face the changes brought about by adolescence. Lindberg (1991) suggested that they have an 'incomplete and confused image of themselves' because they lost – and then perhaps gradually regained, some skills during the years since regression. It was reported that the students in Lindberg's study sometimes enjoyed looking in the mirror, taking pride in new clothes.

Mirror games and photo albums were suggested as possible ways in which to build the girl's awareness of herself and her body.

Emotional development and Rett Syndrome

For many parents the first signs that something is amiss with their daughter are noticeable changes in her emotional well being. She may, towards the end of her first year, have long periods of inexplicable crying, unhappiness and anger. For the first year of her life all may have appeared well and she made apparently 'normal' progress. Close examination of early videos by Kerr (1994) however, shows that the child is affected by Rett Syndrome before regression, but the signs are subtle and not noticeable to the unsuspecting eye.

It is thought that a developmental 'ceiling' is reached at about 9 to 12 months, which will be followed by a regression. At this time unhappiness is apparent, many parents reporting that their daughter cut herself off from personal contact, avoided eye-contact, clung to familiar toys and routines.

Regression

This is a period of chaos in her life when both the girl and those around her are bewildered and confused by her apparent regression. For her, everything is changing. Suddenly things she could do easily have become impossible. Lindberg surmised what she might be feeling:

> Her world is no longer safe and predictable and she no longer knows her way about. She has lost her control and her foothold. Not only has the world changed. Her role in it has changed too. She is no longer the one who knows. She is someone who does not know any more – but she cannot understand why.

> (Lindberg 1991)

As with people everywhere faced with crisis, each child will cope with the regression in her own way. For some the regression may be sudden and severe, for others it may be gentler. Some will take longer to recover, and to come to terms with their new role. For each child with Rett Syndrome, the effects of the regression will be different, depending on her age and the skills she had acquired before it began.

Whatever the nature and length of the regression period, it is well-documented that a long period of calm and stability will follow, which has usually been reached by the time the girl is of the age to enter full-time education.

Expressing emotions

Rett (1986) suggested that girls with Rett Syndrome expressed themselves through various channels in response to simple activity deep in the brain. Their actions reflect this brain activity, through channels such as the stereotypical hand movements, rocking or hyperventilation. He saw these actions as very necessary to the individual, so that, if one channel was blocked (for example, the hand movements being prevented by the use of splints) then in response, another would open (for example, rocking). He saw such movements as an expression of her emotional state. It was suggested that the eyes provide the main point of contact with the girl's feelings.

> I now travel around the world to see these children and I can say that the problems are the same world-wide. I think that the parents' problems are also the same. The children's faces and expressions I see more and more in a philosophical view. I am interested to know what the children can see, what goes into the brain because they are so interesting, sometimes we think the child can see us, sometimes they see straight through us. I think the eyes are the only possible means of contact. I have seen many children, the expression was the same, and they are alive with their eyes.
>
> (Rett 1985)

Rett (1985) warned that establishing contact would not always be easy, sometimes being affected by the feelings of the person attempting to 'reach' the girl. 'The mother is not able to find this contact if she is tired or depressed.'

Music

Music offers the girl with Rett Syndrome opportunities to express her emotions. Rett (1985) felt strongly that music reached to the girl, and that she is sensitive to it. Lindberg (1991) outlined the benefits of music therapy for girls who are so emotional: 'Through music therapy they feel, and in this way come to understand such concepts as time and space, quality and quantity, cause and effect. Their own identity is developed, too.'

Findings from questionnaires and observations

The ways in which emotions are expressed

Data indicated that the most common way the girls expressed their emotions was through their eyes. Laughs and smiles were also widely used, as were facial expressions. Some girls used movement, body language and hands, some used vocalisations.

Direct eye contact may have reduced during the period of regression, but it later seemed to become the main way of expressing emotions. This was evident in girls of all ages, and it appeared that they continued to refine the use of their eyes throughout their lives.

Smiles and laughter were reported as being used to indicate apparent happiness, or to attract attention. It was reported often that a sense of humour was displayed through giggling and laughing, one teacher describing how 'she's lovely when she's happy, with a great sense of humour'. Another, writing of her pupil's personality, said 'she has a generally happy disposition and a good sense of humour', and yet another, by a parent of her 30 year old daughter, 'her eyes sparkle and she smiles'.

Spontaneous laughter, chuckles and giggles were mentioned in relation to apparently favourite activities such as certain TV programmes, videos and tapes. It was also mentioned in response to immediate situations that arose – one example given was when someone else in the class was being told off! Many parents recounted embarrassing anecdotal incidents of giggling and laughing, when she clearly saw the funny side of something others were trying to ignore.

Other facial expressions such as grimacing, looking sad, angry, excited and surprised were all mentioned as ways in which the girls appeared to express their feelings. An identified response to conversation was 'her face lights up when spoken to'.

Despite physical difficulties, most girls demonstrated a range of movements in order to express emotion, for example, turning away and towards, rocking or kicking. For some, any purposeful movement of their bodies was very difficult. For others, able to perform a wide range of movements, it was the control of movements that presented difficulty. Actions such as rocking were reported as becoming violent and possibly injurious when the student became agitated or upset.

The nature and intensity of animation appeared to depend on many factors both within the girl and external to her. Some had excitable, volatile natures, whilst others were more laconic and 'laid back'. Interest, fright, boredom and excitement were all demonstrated by increasing or decreasing animation of particular movements or body language. This was observed and reported to be individual to each girl, and required individual evaluation in order to determine whether she was reacting positively or negatively to a given situation.

There were emotional reactions reported that were described as aggressive. Two girls, when unhappy, were reported to bite, pinch, hit or pull the hair of others or themselves.

It was reported that the stereotypical movements of the hands could reflect the girl's emotions, becoming more intense when she was agitated or excited. This led in some cases to self-injurious behaviour – for example, when hand-wringing became so intense as to lead to a breaking down of the skin. Equally, hand movements sometimes became less intense indicating calmness, slowly relaxing towards sleep.

Vocalisations were described as shouts, squeals, murmurs and grunts. Some of the noises were associated with hyperventilation. It was noted that the occurrence of vocalisations as a means of communication appeared to be more prevalent in those under the age of ten, and that it became less common with age. One girl was observed to use words in response to a set of pictures she was shown.

Unpredictable mood swings were highlighted as a problem for many teachers in planning the girls' educational programmes. One teacher said 'her mood changes dramatically from one day to another and she often becomes upset for no apparent reason'. Teachers accounted for this in various ways. Often it was felt that there was a physical cause and digestive problems were suspected.

The onset of puberty was reported to be a time of emotional difficulty for some girls, when mood swings became very apparent – described as 'powerful' by one teacher. This was reported by teachers of girls of ages that would suggest mood swings can continue throughout adolescence.

It appeared that some girls with Rett Syndrome became tense and anxious, suffered panic attacks and showed signs of great agitation. This often occurred in response to certain situations. One teacher expressed concern when the pupil she was working with showed signs of anxiety in large, echoing rooms, for example, the dining room and swimming pool. This created a dilemma, as swimming had been recommended as part of the educational programme, yet the teacher felt that the anxiety created by the pool negated the benefits of the swimming.

Calming influences

When great agitation was expressed, perhaps by crying or shouting, teachers had usually found one thing that would calm and relax their particular pupil. Sometimes cuddling, close holding and rocking calmed younger children. For older students favourite music was often mentioned, ranging from quiet classical to heavy metal, each individual having her own preferences. Sometimes teachers found the familiarity of a well known favourite video restored her peace of mind. Once again tastes varied widely, from sing-along children's songs and stories, to wild, flashing, noisy, pop videos.

Relaxation
For some girls, especially in the older age range, relaxation was built into their weekly timetable, in one case as part of a leisure option. In a few instances, girls were receiving massage and aromatherapy, which appeared to be much enjoyed by all. One teacher reported that the 'Loving Hands' type of massage had been successful with one particular pupil with Rett Syndrome.

In one special school visited, as part of the schools in-service training programme, several of the nursery nurses had completed a recognised Aromatherapy and Massage course at their local college's Beauty Therapy

Department. The expertise they had acquired was observed to have benefited many of the children at the school, including the girls with Rett Syndrome.

Music therapy

The individual work carried out by music therapists provided examples of music being used to reach the girls' emotions in an exceptionally sensitive and moving way. In the music therapy observed, particularly the individual sessions, the girls' expressions of their feelings were drawn out carefully and responded to by the therapist. There were only a few girls who had this facility available within school, though there were several examples of families paying privately for this service outside school.

Age-appropriate activities

As mentioned, aromatherapy and massage were felt to be particularly important for the older girls in the study. Many teachers felt that finding leisure activities for this age group was particularly difficult. They wished to offer activities that acknowledged the girl as a young lady and not a child, but the girls' severe disabilities limited their access to typical teenage pastimes.

In one mainstream high school visited, a girl with Rett Syndrome worked alongside her peers in Cosmetology (the art of applying make-up). Support was provided by other girls in the group or by an assistant.

Emotional support

Familiar staff and established routines were reported as encouraging emotional stability, allowing the student to feel secure within her environment and aware of what was happening. Teachers were observed first thing in the morning discussing with the group the pattern the day would take. That day's timetable was often illustrated on the wall using photographs and symbols. Before each change of activity, what was going to happen next was carefully and simply explained again to the individual.

In a class of six young ladies with Rett Syndrome, it was noticed that the teacher used a calm and even tone of voice when addressing each one in her class. Requests were clear, the language used brief, but appropriate. Repetition was often necessary and was delivered in the same even tone, using the same language. Responses were gradually and gently coaxed, and success acknowledged and praised in the same quiet tone. This particular group of girls appeared to respond very well to the calm, firm approach of their teacher and the atmosphere it created in their classroom.

Knowledge of the girl and Rett Syndrome

It was observed that some teachers responded intuitively to their individual pupil's emotional needs. They could sense when she was becoming unhappy and redirect her attention to restore her peace of mind. Such teachers could quickly gauge the girl's mood, and knew immediately whether or not a planned activity was appropriate to her current emotional state. These teachers knew their pupil very well indeed and in some cases had been working with her for a long time. Some teachers had made strenuous efforts to form relationships with the pupil's parents, finding out what she particularly liked and disliked in order to be able to read her individual emotional signs.

With no reliable way of determining her exact feelings, careful observation may serve to illustrate the different ways in which each girl with Rett Syndrome expresses her emotions. Recognition of these feelings allows her to directly influence what is going on around her. Acknowledging how she feels about aspects of her life affords her the respect and dignity to which she is entitled.

Strategies to promote emotional well-being are outlined in the final chapter.

Chapter 4

Intellectual Factors

The concept of intelligence has a history of controversy – sometimes viewed as a measurable quality in an individual, like height, or as an 'inheritance' possessed in varying degrees. The wealth of developmental assessments available show measured peaks and troughs of skills and abilities, based on the norms of child development.

Prior to 1971, pupils thought to have an IQ of less than 50 were assumed to be ineducable, and were not included in the education system (Sebba *et al.* 1993). An extension of IQ and diagnostic testing was the use of psychometric tests. However, it has become clear that these procedures are of questionable validity and reliability.

For girls with Rett Syndrome, most of these developmentally-based measures used with children with severe or profound learning difficulties pre-suppose that developmental milestones will be reached in broadly the right order, albeit severely delayed. However, very many milestones require a growing dexterity and increasing exploration of objects and the environment – picking things up; transferring things from one hand to the other; moving around to explore; posting things; imitating actions. Some girls will be able to demonstrate some of these skills, but because of their specific disabilities, such achievements are going to be atypical or impossible for many and, therefore, no true indicator of intellectual potential.

Intellectual development and communication

A child's intellectual development and their communication skills are inextricably linked. Language acquisition will usually be slow, where there are learning difficulties, and the lack of speech in turn affects intellectual development. Few pupils in schools for pupils with severe or complex learning difficulties, therefore, have typical speech or language skills.

Kiernan *et al.* (1987) defined communication as 'responses which a person makes intentionally in order to affect the behaviour of another person and with the expectation that the other person will receive and act on that message'. These responses, then, will include speaking, listening, sign language, symbol vocabularies, as well as non-verbal elements of communicative interaction such as gesture, expression and body language.

For any pupil with profound learning disabilities, the challenge for professionals is in providing a curriculum for individuals whose levels of communication may appear no higher than a few weeks (Mitre, in Coupe and Goldbart 1988).

Leeming *et al.* (1979) suggested that communication need not solely rely on learning, but that 'we are born with a considerable number of "wired-in" programmes to communicate'. These authors felt that to describe any child as 'non-communicating' was a contradiction in terms.

Jones and Cregan (1986) considered communication difficulties to be one of the most significant disabilities of all. Not to teach an alternative form of communication, they argued, excluded that person from any major involvement in their society, limited their intellectual development and hindered their educational progress.

Kiernan (1988) described the development of communication skills as central to the social, emotional and cognitive development of these pupils. Banes (in Aherne and Thornber, 1990) went further, describing the right to express needs, make decisions and choices, and participate within a group as a basic human right.

There is little researched and documented information on the intellectual potential of girls with Rett Syndrome – many hypotheses are based on observation and anecdotal evidence. However, most agree that prior to regression and diagnosis, they follow broadly typical milestones in their development, although in retrospect these milestones may have been incomplete or delayed.

Kerr (1986) outlined the time course of Rett Syndrome, and stated that girls are generally considered normal at birth and for the first six months of life. She described 'a ceiling of development at the 10–12 month stage, beyond which the child is not equipped to pass'. At around 12 months (between 6 and 30 months) a period of regression begins and skills are lost. Commonly, a girl enters a phase of screaming and anxiety and withdraws from social contact. Where she has acquired speech, she will usually lose it around this time. By the end of this period, which may last for a few days or many months, it is clear that the girl is profoundly disabled.

Kerr suggested that all sufferers demonstrate a level of skill under that expected at one year. However, she also estimated that their understanding of communication is 'not less than the 12 month level'. She also described how some girls may retain a few useful words which may suddenly, and aptly, be produced years later.

Owing to the girls' difficulty in making sense of sights and sounds, their slow reaction time and their severely disabled movements, Kerr recommended assessment methods which were independent of voluntary movement.

Naidu (undated) agreed with this early history, also describing the period of inconsolable screaming, combined with poor interaction. Once this phase was over, Naidu portrayed quiet, placid girls with eye-contact as their main, or only, means of communication.

Witt Engerstrom (1990) described the condition of Rett Syndrome from a neurodevelopmental perspective, and suggested that the syndrome may be a disorder sequentially involving selected neural mechanisms crucial for development. She advised that these children are unable to move from the sensory motor stage of development into the symbolic level of maturation. She also described the phase after regression as an 'awakening', during which contact and communication improved as the girls made efforts to use their eyes to compensate for their apraxic hands.

Lindberg (1991) described a regression of development in reasoning, communication and social skills, and considered that the females within her study all operated within the first 18 months of development. She outlined situations in which they identified and remembered situations, but believed that they have difficulty in generalising that knowledge to new situations. Lindberg highlighted the difficulty in being exact about the girls' comprehension, as they are unable to 'prove' their apparent skills through speech, actions or following directions. 'Action in itself is not the entire skill, and absence of action does not necessarily mean absence of knowledge' (Lindberg 1991).

Lindberg also described her work using pictures with girls with Rett Syndrome. She felt that almost all those in her study showed great interest in pictures, photographs and television. Many had learned to associate a picture with a real object, and some could interpret new and unfamiliar pictures.

Field (1990), a parent of a daughter with Rett Syndrome, urged us not to refer back to comparisons of 'normality', as he believed that the child with Rett Syndrome has 'a different order of experience that is fragile and easily disturbed, yet coherent for all that'.

Findings from observations and questionnaires

Several teachers highlighted the difficulties in accurately assessing the girls' intellectual skills: 'I feel strongly that the assessments and checklists we use do not give credit for her personality and skills' and 'she presents as a child who should be beyond "experiencing" and should now be "exploring", but she cannot sustain or co-ordinate intention with action'.

Almost half the teachers interviewed considered that working on cognitive skills was a major priority for their pupil with Rett Syndrome.

Speech and language therapist – research institute, USA

A speech therapist was interviewed, who had responsibility for evaluating and assessing the communication skills of girls with Rett Syndrome. It was her opinion that although expressive skills (e.g. speech / signing) in the girls are poorly developed, this is less evident in their receptive skills (understanding). She described the problems that girls with Rett Syndrome have in initiating activities, not only from one day to another, but also from one session to another. This therapist had met two girls with speech, one of whom used sentences and another with 30 spontaneous words and 60 words that she understood. This girl was beginning to put two words together. Other girls she had met were capable of occasionally saying an odd word when particularly happy or frustrated. Amongst the girls known to this therapist were two who used sign language, each having three signs.

Specialist class, residential community, USA

This residential and educational community provided for people with special needs from school age through to old age, offering appropriate educational and vocational opportunities. This facility had close links with the research institute, above.

Within a school for pupils with Severe Learning Difficulties, a special class had been set up to cater for six students with Rett Syndrome, between the ages of 13 and 19 years old. The class teacher had organised the room in order to facilitate communication in her students with Rett Syndrome, to encourage them to exercise choice and make demands. Areas of the room had been set up to allow access to the types of activities the teacher felt would motivate her students, e.g. books, tapes, drinks. Many of the students were observed approaching particular areas to choose activities, and others were assisted to these areas and their reactions noted and acted upon.

The students were observed interacting with each other – looking, laughing and touching. The pace and style of all the lessons allowed ample opportunity for the students with Rett Syndrome to demonstrate their ability to participate, make demands, have fun.

Communication survey on 12 girls with Rett Syndrome

This survey set out to establish the many ways in which girls with Rett Syndrome communicate. Almost all the pupils were described as happy by their teachers, and half of them were considered to respond positively to familiar people. Some had particular difficulty in dealing with unfamiliar settings or new people. All of them used facial expression, smiles and laughs to indicate how they were feeling or that they were enjoying themselves.

Three quarters of the girls used eye-contact in order to initiate social contact with other people, or in order to choose food or activities. Some used other means in order to make choices, such as scanning followed by a strong eye-gaze, tapping preferred items, or perhaps simply opening their mouth if they liked a particular food.

Their most consistent means of communication was by using their eyes – looking at people or objects, fleetingly or staring hard, and closing their eyes or turning away when bored or uninterested. All the girls used vocalisations, laughing, crying, shouting or generally making sounds, according to their mood.

A further strength for all of them was in their use of body movements, perhaps moving towards something or someone, or conversely, rocking vigorously away from things! All except two could touch, pat, swipe or knock anything which interested them.

Three quarters of the girls would look at pictures on request, and half of them could also touch a picture when asked to. Four could look at symbols appropriately – one could eye-point to yes/no symbol cards to indicate her feelings and needs.

A range of communication skills were apparent with Rett Syndrome pupils. They could all indicate likes and dislikes, comfort and discomfort and feelings of being sad or happy. They could all use their eyes to show their teachers and carers their preferences in the 'here and now'. Some of them had refined these skills to a more abstract level, recognising pictures or symbols to represent other possibilities which were visible at that time. One girl could nod or shake her head to answer 'yes' or 'no'. Although this was a very small survey, involving only 12 subjects, it serves to indicate some of the broad ways in which girls with Rett Syndrome do communicate their ideas and thoughts.

Results from the Pre-Verbal Communication Schedule on 16 girls

The PVCS identifies pre-communicative and communication skills in pupils who do not speak.

Pre-communicative behaviours

All the girls had well-defined needs and preferences, which is an essential skill in having something to communicate about. These related to events – such as trips in a car, baths, spending time with other people and music. Many also had favourite toys and foods. They could all express their preferences and influence their lives accordingly.

All the girls were reported as visually proficient at this level, having a blinking reflex and being able to fixate on an object. Most could turn and look at an object, track a moving object and look from one feature to another on someone's face. Many girls showed interest in books, pictures and catalogues, and could recognise visual clues by choosing favourite foods or recognising people from a distance. A few could sort and match pictures visually and recognise people in photographs.

Most of the girls were able to release objects, and many could grasp and hold objects. Few could use their hands in normal everyday movements, and no-one could use fingers for finer movements.

All the girls showed significant interest in other people and were socially responsive – e.g. watching others with interest, smiling, showing excitement. Most could initiate eye-contact with other people and enjoyed close physical contact with familiar people.

Each of the girls had well-developed listening skills demonstrated by looking at someone who was talking to her, and turning her head to look in the direction of sounds or someone talking or singing. Most changed their body movements in response to another person's voice and would stop crying in reaction to voices or music. Most, too, reacted differently to varied tones of voice and could bang or hit musical toys or instruments in order to make sounds.

Most of the girls were able to make sounds spontaneously, from grunts/moans to vowel or mmm/sss sounds. A few girls could repeat sounds (ma-ma-ma), combine sounds (da-ba; ee-ah) or babble. Two children in the study occasionally used single words.

Most of the girls were reported to breathe, chew and swallow normally. Three could suck through a straw, but none could blow.

All the girls laughed or smiled when relaxed or happy, and most of them cried when in pain or distress. Most could also express their anger by squeals or shouts, and some could hit out at another person in anger or frustration. Two could kiss other people as part of a social routine.

Almost all the girls listened to music with clear evidence of enjoyment. A few could beat or tap along with music, and dance by swaying back and forth. No-one was able to hum or sing.

Imitative skills

One or two girls could imitate certain motor movements, such as clapping hands, tapping the table or waving goodbye. However, for most, little success was achieved in this area.

Two or three girls could imitate vocalisations such as speech noises, each imitating her own noises from a cassette tape, blowing a raspberry, or imitating sounds of distress from other people.

Informal communicative behaviours

No-one could physically show or give an object to another person on request. A few girls, however, used objects or pictures to communicate. One could approach an object – e.g. a cup – if she wanted a drink. Seven could indicate a picture of a preferred or needed item, using a strong eye-gaze or touching / tapping.

Almost all could stiffen arms and legs in order to resist an activity, and many could refuse to move or cooperate if the mood took them.

Five girls could indicate 'no' by shaking the head, or in one case pursing the lips. Two could nod their heads for 'yes'. One could wave goodbye consistently.

Most of the girls could approach or touch another person in order to gain attention, and half of them could push people away if they did not want interference. Most of the girls could, at least some of the time, touch something they wanted. Only four combined this with glancing between the object and a person, while touching, as a way of 'asking'. Fourteen girls consistently looked at things they wanted, and all but one could look back and forth between the object and a person until they were responded to.

Many of the girls could use sounds in order to gain attention, although this was seldom with varying intonation or if people were out of sight. A few used particular noises when objecting, and one could take turns with another person when making sounds. Many girls shouted when frustrated and could also scowl or frown when displeased. A few used kisses as an expression of affection. There were virtually no reported incidences of girls provoking others through their behaviour, although one girl was reported as aggressive to others in various situations.

Formal communicative behaviours

Many of the girls could take another person's hand when it was held out to them, and could also 'look' when someone was pointing to an object. Most would look away or close their eyes if they did not want to look 'on command'. Most did not follow instructions to look at objects several metres away, or follow gestures such as 'come here' used without speech. Thirteen girls could respond to their own names consistently. Most understood when told 'no'. A few responded to standard phrases such as 'sit down', 'come here' etc. A few could indicate several familiar people on photographs by using a strong eye-gaze. None of the girls could show any body parts on request. A few girls were reported as finding it very funny if someone else was in trouble!

Many of the girls were reported as communicating through photos or symbols. Many others were working on this. One girl used 15–20 symbols and 20–25 pictures or photos in order to make choices or communicate her needs. Two girls used one sign each and two others used occasional words.

The many ways described give a good indication of the girl with Rett Syndrome's means of expressing her thoughts and ideas. Each will have enormous difficulty communicating and demonstrating her intellectual capabilities. However, in seeking to help her find alternative channels, the teacher can enable her to influence her life for the better.

Field (1990) argued that the assumption that all girls with Rett Syndrome are functioning at 'some kind of infantile mental level' is a very over-simplified generalisation:

> What can you deduce of (her) intelligence, for instance, when she has such a passionate love and awareness of music, particularly Bob Dylan's, that I can calm her in extreme situations by merely reciting a line or two from a Dylan song? She can communicate her joy for music, for having stories read to her, for water play, for interaction with other people on her own terms, for the exhilaration of a brisk wheelchair ride across Vauxhall Bridge, but she cannot communicate the whys and wherefores of the process. Science cannot put such anecdotal, intuitive data through any kind of test, and it seems, therefore, that the whole question must remain open.

Strategies to promote intellectual development are described in the final chapter.

Part 2

The Specific Barriers to Learning in Rett Syndrome

Teachers, having considered the physical, social, emotional and intellectual factors that influence each individual girl, will need to look at the barriers to learning presented by the syndrome itself. These barriers are present in all with a diagnosis of Rett Syndrome, and are:

1. Hand dysfunction
2. Delayed or atypical response
3. Apraxia

(Lewis and Wilson 1991)

The challenges presented by these specific difficulties will vary for each individual, depending on how she is affected by the syndrome. It is important that the three barriers are recognised by all working with her, and that planning is focused to try and overcome them.

The effects of the barriers may vary greatly from one day to the next, due to the influence and interplay of physical, social, emotional or intellectual factors. For example, if she is feeling unhappy, uncomfortable or insecure, then it is harder for her to summon the motivation necessary to overcome her apraxia and her hand movements may also intensify. Thus the barriers intensify, feeding from each other and the combination of the physical, social, emotional and intellectual factors that affect her. Learning, in this situation, becomes very difficult.

The three barriers, and how they may affect the person with Rett Syndrome will be looked at in more detail on the following pages.

Chapter 5

Hand Dysfunction

The constant movement of the hands in a stereotypical way is immediately apparent when meeting someone affected by Rett Syndrome:

> The leading symptom of stereotypy enables relatively quick recognition of the children who spend virtually the whole of their waking period in a striking fashion, rubbing, kneading or 'beating' their hands.
>
> Rett (1968)

Since there is, as yet, no organic 'marker' for Rett Syndrome, diagnosis is made on clinical observation, and evidence of repetitive hand movements is one of the criteria on which diagnosis is made (Kerr 1987).

The movements begin to emerge following the period of regression, so are first noticed between one and three years of age (Milne 1990). They continue throughout life, although they tend to slow down with increasing age. Lindberg (1991) and Van Acker (1991) observed that the person's age and their environment affected both the frequency and duration of the stereotypical movements. It was also reported that attempts to reduce or stop the movements using various medications had been unsuccessful. (Percy *et al.* 1985 in Van Acker 1991).

The nature of hand dysfunction

Hand movements vary with each person, and are individual to her. They have been described in various ways. Hagberg et al. (1983) mentioned 'hand-washing' movements in front of the mouth or chest, rubbing of hands and blows to teeth. In addition to this description, Lindberg (1991) described picking or clasping movements, further observing hand-to-mouth and hand-to-body movements, i.e. hands to face, chest or shoulder, and the involvement of both hands separately. Wilson (1992) added wringing, clapping and tapping, and the development of a complicated individual pattern of hand and arm movement.

Precisely why these movements are made is not known, but it is an integral part of the syndrome. Professor Rett (1985) explained his thoughts on the origins of the movements, believing that they were made in response to activity deep in the brain, and that they were unique to each individual. It was also reported that the hand movements appeared to act as a 'discharge for some inner tension' (Hodgkinson 1987). This was further reported by Lindberg (1991) who surmised that they were 'channelling a need for motion', that the girl felt her hands 'strange' in some way, and that the movements overcame this sense of strangeness.

How the hand movements affect learning

Although the reason for the complex hand movements is not known, their effect is clear to the observer. Milne (1990) explained that they invariably stopped the child using her hands for any constructive purpose – that 'the hands behave as if they are no longer under voluntary control'.

The presence of a constant complex movement of both hands obviously affects the person in all aspects of her life and most students with Rett Syndrome have little or no purposeful hand-use. Sharpe (1992) observed that no functional grasp was evident, and that frequently a pincer grasp was not used at all. It was noted by Lindberg that it was not only the action of the hands which prevented her using them purposefully, but that she became totally self-absorbed in their movements. This led to increasing action, and more self absorption – a vicious circle.

The compulsion of the movements appears to override other demands made on the student. Lindberg suggested that certain stimuli would interest her enough to moderate the stereotypical movements temporarily. Such stimuli would be different for individuals, but there was a noticeable slowing down of the movements whenever she became fascinated by something else. This needed to be gauged carefully though, since something too interesting and exciting overstimulated her, and the movements intensified further in response to excitement. Van Acker (1991) reported the apparent success of music therapy in keeping the child more involved with her environment, encouraging her to interact and to use her hands to participate.

Restraint of the hand movements

There are reported instances where the nature of the stereotypical movements was harmful (Lindberg 1991). Such examples occurred where the movements involved the person hitting herself hard, or when constant tapping around the mouth led to soreness. As can be imagined, meal times have also been identified as a time when the hand movements caused difficulties.

It has therefore been necessary to find ways to modify the hand movements in certain situations. Sometimes, holding hands gently was found to be sufficient, and sometimes being placed prone stopped the movements. It was reported that the girls seemed to find it 'relaxing and quieting' to have the stereotypical behaviour stopped in such ways (Sharpe 1992).

The use of splints

Splints, and the use of other restraints, have been investigated by various researchers in the field of occupational therapy. In 1988 Naganuma and Billingsley tested the effectiveness of hand splints in three patients with Rett Syndrome. They concluded that the splints were somewhat effective in reducing the hand-movements and skin breakdown. However, Van Acker (1991) found that improvements in hand use due to splints had not been maintained in any study, and noted that some people with Rett Syndrome were unable to tolerate splints.

Sharpe (1992) used elbow splints in a small scale study, and reported that stereotypical hand movements were reduced, and toy contact increased. More recently Brown, an occupational therapist working in Oregon USA in 1994, stressed the importance of establishing the dominant hand in both the stereotypical movements, and other actions.

Throughout the available literature it is emphasised that the use of splints should be undertaken sensitively. Rett (1985) suggested that splints should only be used for part of the day, since he felt that the movements provided a necessary outlet for the girl's emotions, and that, if her arms were stopped, her feelings would come out another way – e.g. hyperventilation, rocking etc. Milne (1990) suggested that it was frustrating and could be harmful to the child to use splints for very long periods of time.

The importance of occupational therapy

In the planning and carrying out of programmes to increase the hand use of a person with Rett Syndrome, the occupational therapist has a vital part to play. Hanks (1990) reported that success was achieved using techniques that reinforced behaviours that were incompatible with the hand movements. It was suggested that trying to stop the hand movements increased the patient's anxiety, and so it became harder to overcome. By encouraging her to do something she wanted to, something that could not be done while engaged in the movements, the patient herself would overcome them to some extent.

More recent research (Piazza *et al.* 1993) asserted that some functional hand-use could be re-acquired using prompts and reinforcements. In their study of five girls with Rett Syndrome, varying improvements were noted in self-feeding skills over a period of intensive training. This appeared to be maintained when followed up two and a half years later. The researchers in this study suggested that further work could discover if the evident increase in self-feeding skills led to an increase in overall hand-use.

Planned hand use programmes would appear to present a possible way through this barrier to learning, but it was reported that just four per cent of girls in the PSAUK receive any occupational therapy (Cass 1994). A similar lack of occupational therapy was also noted in Sweden by Barbro Lindberg in 1991.

Findings from questionnaires and observations

Lack of hand-use was highlighted as a major challenge to be overcome by a great number of teachers. The difficulties presented by a lack of hand use were described in several ways. One teacher described her pupils' 'twiddling' as an 'inappropriate behaviour'. Another said 'her hand movements impede learning experiences and necessary skills'.

Some recognised that the hand movements related to other factors. One teacher felt that they were strongly related to her motivation, and found it a challenge to overcome her 'reluctance to use her hands'. Another expressed the view that hyperventilation was linked to hand movements, and that constituted a double hurdle.

45

Observation of girls illustrated a vast variation of hand use. Many had basic whole-arm movements, such as swiping and knocking. These could be used to some effect in certain situations, the most common being knocking a plate of food or a cup to apparently indicate a need for a drink or food. Others could manage a gentle tap if something was near enough to them.

One young lady with Rett Syndrome had retained her fine motor skills to the extent that she was observed picking raisins from a small pot and eating them. This particular girl had received intensive occupational therapy support from an early age.

Occupational therapy

Increasing hand use was mentioned often by teachers as a teaching priority, yet it was found in the study that very few girls received occupational therapy in the UK. In the United States and Canada, where occupational therapy was identified as an educational need, personnel and time allocated was specified in the girls' Individual Education Plans.

Tests

Teachers recognised that the lack of hand use meant that the achievement of their pupils could not properly be reflected in test and check-list data, since the tests themselves related strongly to hand use, for example posting shapes.

Equipment

Teachers frequently mentioned their difficulty in obtaining suitable classroom equipment either with which to work on developing hand use, or which was accessible, given their limitations. This was highlighted as an increasing problem as the students grew older, in that their teachers wished them to work with age-appropriate materials.

An element of surprise was found to motivate some students, and some teachers used toys that not only surprised, but also made them laugh. Such toys had been found in unexpected places, not necessarily obtained through expensive specialist educational suppliers. Market stalls, pet shops, car boot sales were trawled for the unusual by inventive teachers, who then individually adapted items to suit their pupil and her particular likes.

Computers

Computers with touch-screens, sound beams, pads and joy-sticks, all sensitive to the slightest intentional movement, were observed being used by several students with Rett Syndrome. Programs that stimulated a quick response, rewarding the slightest effort with music and an array of brightly-coloured images, were reported to have achieved success.

Music

Music was often successfully used by teachers to motivate the student to use her hands purposefully. The intensive individual work of the music therapist was observed to lead to exploration of the creative use of the hands, and so to overcome temporarily the demands of the stereotypical movements. The therapists observed used a variety of instruments dependent upon each individual's preference.

Music in group situations was also observed to motivate and to encourage hand use, students using their hands to take their turn at the instrument. It was evident in one music lesson observed with six students with Rett Syndrome, that they paid great attention not only to the therapist, but also to each other when participating. While someone was being sung to, to encourage her to play her part, the others listened and watched intently, all hand movements reduced, anticipating their turn.

Teachers had made their own musical instruments that created immediate and varied responses to the slightest intentional touch. Some musical effects were created using the stereotypical movements themselves, teachers making mittens and wrist bands with bells and other sound effects responsive to the individuals' pattern of movement.

Sensory work

Sensory experiences of various other kinds were used by teachers as diversions from the stereotypical hand movements. Water was used in various ways, and a few teachers had developed the use of this medium by using colours, bubbles, soaps or perfumes in the water to add extra sensory dimensions to further motivate. Teachers encouraged the use of fingers to create images in finger paint, shaving foam and other art mediums.

Restraint of the hand movements

It was reported by their teachers that many girls disliked having their hands touched, and actively objected to having their special rhythms interfered with. This created a dilemma for many teachers, as they wished to encourage the use of hands purposefully, yet realised that the movements were of deep importance to their pupils.

Splints were used by some teachers for certain activities. Some teachers gently restrained the hands when wishing the pupil to attend to something else. This appeared effective when the teacher was talking to the pupil, but then greatly restricted how much physical assistance the teacher could give to enable the student to complete the task.

One teacher had made rice bags for her particular pupil's wrists. These were just heavy enough to prevent her becoming absorbed in the stereotypical movements, yet light enough that she felt comfortable with them and so was able to participate in the table-top activity.

The final chapter of this book outlines strategies to promote hand function.

Chapter 6

Delayed Response

Those affected by Rett Syndrome show a delayed response to stimuli of all kinds. This presents a major barrier to their learning that must be recognised by all who work with them, since it is possible to misinterpret this delay as an inability to respond. This misinterpretation would be damaging to the child's self esteem, and could lead to her loss of motivation, as her efforts to respond are 'missed'.

The barrier to learning presented by the delayed response in those with Rett Syndrome, has been described by several researchers; for example, Lindberg (1990 and 1991) and Lewis and Wilson (1991). The need for staff to recognise the difficulties it presents in learning are further emphasised and described in IRSA 1990:

> Another common concern when working with children with Rett Syndrome is their delayed response pattern, a significant period of time between when a request is made and when the child is able to respond. We believe that the delayed response should be expected and planned for in programming.
>
> (Murphy and Barrett in IRSA 1990)

Lindberg (1991) made reference to a delayed response to pain, as observed by many parents in her study. It can be argued that if a delayed response to such a strong stimulus as pain is evident, then a delay is to be expected in response to other stimuli.

During this time lapse, between stimulus and response, Lindberg suggested that several things are happening within the student. She may be assessing and weighing up a situation before she feels that she wants to become a part of it. She may not be able to act as soon as she feels that she wants to.

In order to deal with this, Lindberg suggested that those working with the pupil must allow her lots of time, yet remain alert in order to capitalise on the response when it comes. She will then be encouraged by realising that her efforts, however small, are recognised. For this to occur distraction must be minimal, since a seemingly small distraction can mean that the whole process will have to begin again.

It has been observed that distraction may mean the loss of opportunity. Some students affected by Rett Syndrome tend to tire easily and their concentration and attention become harder to focus as time goes on. If this happens, Lindberg suggested allowing the student a time of quiet, in order that she may 'recharge her batteries' and then trying again later. It was also suggested that the learning environment of the girl is structured so as to minimise the possibility of any distraction.

How delayed response affects learning

The delayed response is an aspect of the condition and, whatever is happening inside, whatever its cause and purpose, it is an integral part of the pupil. The way in which it affects learning is dependent on the teacher's response to it.

If time is not allowed for the response, then there is the possibility that the great effort needed on the student's part to react appropriately will be missed, and she will have lost the opportunity to achieve success. Conversely, if the appropriate time can be given, the teacher awaiting a response in the state of 'calm alertness' described by Lindberg, then success may be achieved and the student further encouraged to repeat her actions.

Findings from questionnaires and observations

Delayed response was present in all students involved in the study, and several teachers saw it as the major challenge in the teaching of girls with Rett Syndrome.

Variations in delayed response

The nature of the delayed response varied, and it was reported that in individuals themselves it differed from day to day. It was described and observed to be as long as several minutes, and as short as a few seconds.

In some students it was observed that eye contact was maintained, and they appeared to be attending. In others it appeared almost as if requests had not been heard or understood, since they carried on uninterrupted in their stereotypical behaviours or hyperventilation during the response time. Although she appeared unaware of what was required, it seemed that the girl could be drawing on all her resources to overcome her apraxia and stereotypical behaviour in order to respond appropriately.

Focusing attention

It was reported by teachers that great difficulty was experienced in focusing the student's attention. This indicates the nature of the barrier to learning since, as with any child, unless they are attending, learning cannot take place. In one class of six girls with Rett Syndrome the teacher worked individually with one girl at a time, talking quietly and firmly, repeating requests until the girl was attending fully.

Time

Teachers commented on the difficulties they experienced in giving her the time required. It was recognised that time was needed in order to prepare the student for the activity; to focus attention; to allow for delayed response; and then for her to respond appropriately. Alongside this, the teacher may be recording the girl's response in order to monitor and plan progression.

The difficulties of allocating intensive individual time in a busy classroom schedule cannot be overestimated, and were highlighted frequently by the teachers in the study. All of the students in the study received one-to-one teaching for some of their school day, and several were allocated individual support assistance, over and above that which was allocated to the group.

One girl was allowed her 'own time' with a member of staff in a quiet area. The pupil was expected to 'lead' the session, the assistant commenting on what she observed, talking about it, allowing the girl control and choice.

Repetition

Several teachers used computers to encourage the repetition of simple actions. One particular child, observed using a computer joy-stick, had learnt to repeat the simple movement so quickly that the delayed response had been overcome and she successfully achieved her reward of the music and pictures she enjoyed.

Knowledge of the girl

Staff who knew the individual pupil well were observed intuitively adapting to her response time. Eye contact was observed to be maintained, and the student was allowed just enough time to respond. The instructional language used by the staff was controlled, and repeated as often as was necessary to achieve success.

Teachers and support staff, with time and a thorough knowledge of the girl and her condition, can assess just the right moment to challenge her. They will develop an instinct for just how much reaction time to give her. They will learn to read her signs, and so help her overcome this barrier to her learning.

Strategies to minimise delayed response are suggested in the final chapter.

Chapter 7

Apraxia

Apraxia is one of the most fundamental handicaps associated with Rett Syndrome. It affects everything the person tries to do in all aspects of her life – like a cloud, shrouding all her intentions.

Apraxia is a difficulty also experienced by many other children with profound and multiple learning difficulties. It has been described by Sacks (1985) as 'motor bewilderment', and by Williams (1988), as 'an inability to carry out voluntary purposeful movements when there is no paralysis or defect of muscular co-ordination'.

Lindberg (1991) described 'an inability or difficulty in carrying out purposeful movements and actions, in spite of normal mobility'. She went on to further describe how she feels that the girls observed in her study very much wanted to act, but had forgotten how.

The lack of purposeful action was further described by Lewis and Wilson (1991). It appears that the girl has lost the means of controlling her actions. She may be unable to control their strength and speed, so that, for example, an intended tap may end up as a wild swipe.

In an early paper describing Rett Syndrome, Rett (1977) mentioned apraxia as being present in the lower limbs, and evident in the strange gait of the sufferers' walking pattern. He outlined that, in those he studied, their legs were physically capable of walking normally, yet they were unable to do so. He described this as apraxic since the normal walking pattern was disordered in the brain itself.

Lindberg (1991) described verbal apraxia, when the girl attempted to use speech, but was unable to. It was noted that the chewing mechanisms were also affected.

The physical manifestations of apraxia were further recognised by Kjoerholt and Salthammer (in IRSA 1990). They suggested that apraxia be taken into account when devising a programme of physiotherapy for the patient with Rett Syndrome. 'Weak signals from her body' were described and it was recognised that the therapist must give time for the individual to surmount the apraxia.

Apraxia was seen as increasing in a demanding situation, leading to withdrawal if it became necessary to think too hard. Kjoerholt and Salthammer concurred with Lindberg, in that the more practised the movement, the easier it became. Conversely, should the student need to think about the action, then apraxia would take over, resulting in her becoming unable to move the parts of the body required.

How apraxia affects learning

The most obvious effect of apraxia evident to those who work with the girl manifests itself as 'the more she tries, the harder it gets'. The person may be studying her food, may reach out to get it, and the action somehow comes out wrongly. Instead of touching the food, she hits the plate so hard that it shoots off the table. This may then be wrongly interpreted as her not wanting it, and so further add to her frustration. It was suggested by Lindberg (1991) that apraxia can affect many aspects of emotional development and self-esteem.

Lindberg (1991) also described how apraxia brings in all other learning difficulties. The student may be watching something intently, a drink for example; focusing her energy to touch it, thinking hard. As her concentration increases, her hand movements intensify; her hyper-ventilation increases; she may also rock backwards and forwards in her desire to act. Then, the apraxia makes it likely that when she finally does act, her actions are clumsy and uncoordinated.

Findings from questionnaires and observations

Definition

One finding in the data was a clear definition of how apraxia manifests itself in those with Rett Syndrome, as observed by a teacher: 'dithering – like a nervous tension, which can seem to increase with her own desire to do something – and with environmental distractions.'

It was indicated that teachers viewed apraxia as a major challenge in their teaching of these pupils.

Motivation

Teachers reported that motivating the students to try new things caused problems. It was commented that the pupil would often play with old favourite toys and apparatus for a long time, rather than try new ones. It was also reported that the pupil might resist involvement, showing agitation, or she might passively choose not to participate in the activity.

Intention

One teacher described how her particular pupil was 'unable to sustain / co-ordinate intention with action'.

Whilst those with Rett Syndrome may initially feel that they can carry out an action, as soon as they attempt to do so then the apraxia intervenes, preventing them sustaining their original positive thoughts, confusing the issue. This inability to coordinate thought and action was observed on several occasions.

Increasing hand and body movements were observed to result in the eventual action differing from her apparent intention. Teachers had adapted equipment in order that activities were made easier for their pupil. When wild uncoordinated movements were made, teachers clamped bowls and toys to tables in order that their pupils could achieve success.

It was observed that these pupils found difficulty performing more than one activity at a time. One girl was clearly observed to be unable to walk and listen at the same time. She needed to stop walking in order to listen. Another example was seen when one child lifted a drink to her mouth – as she opened her mouth she dropped the cup. It appeared that the simultaneous actions of holding the cup, and opening her mouth were too much for her to cope with together. One teacher had got over this problem by providing a drinking cup made from a carefully shaped cut up container, in order to make it easier for the particular girl to both hold the cup and to drink from it simultaneously.

It was observed that purposeful action is greatly affected by apraxia – actions the girl has to think about. In teaching and learning situations purposeful action indicates to the teacher that the child is understanding. Apraxia was seen to be a barrier to her learning not only in the sense that her actions are severely limited by it, but also by the fact that it prevents her demonstrating that learning has taken place.

Apraxia is a barrier to learning in Rett Syndrome that is not directly observable but appears to affect not only actions, but also motivation and self-esteem. It cannot be photographed and analysed like the hand movements, or timed and measured like the delayed response. Its effect on the girl herself, however, can be observed and sensed by those who know her well, who can recognise and sympathise with her overwhelming efforts to overcome it.

Strategies to minimise the effects of apraxia are suggested in the final chapter.

Part 3

Implications for Teachers

Having looked at the special educational needs of the particular girl with Rett Syndrome and considered the barriers the syndrome presents to her learning, three important implications emerge for teachers' consideration.

Attitudes and values

The first is the question – Why? Why educate children who can't talk, often can't walk and are able to do very little for themselves? What is the point?

In order to answer this question, attitudes towards the education of children with profound and multiple learning difficulties, and the value placed on it by society and their parents, need to be considered by teachers. Each individual needs to consider their own personal attitudes towards their work and its value.

Curriculum

Teachers also need to know what is expected of them in teaching these children. What curriculum must they follow? Much of the National Curriculum is inaccessible to pupils with Rett Syndrome, but there are parts in all the subjects that have relevance to their education. As special schools have grown over the last twenty years, a developmental curriculum has evolved. Elements of this will be important in the programme of the pupil with Rett Syndrome, alongside her additional curriculum designed to meet her particular and individual needs.

Specific strategies

Teachers need to have their own ideas about teaching girls with Rett Syndrome. The strategies suggested in this section may offer a starting point. They have been drawn from detail elsewhere in the book, as they appeared to meet the girls' social, emotional, or intellectual needs, or offer possible ways of overcoming the three described barriers to their learning.

Chapter 8

Attitudes and Values

The attitudes towards, and the values placed on education will greatly affect the quality of that education – no-one can operate in a vacuum. If education is seen as a two-way process between teacher and child, then the attitude of the teacher to the education of that particular child, and the value she places on it will be vital contributors to its success.

All children look to those around them when forming their own sets of values. Those with Rett Syndrome have special educational needs, and experience the profound and multiple learning difficulties that are part of the syndrome, but they are children and young people first.

It can be argued that the attitudes of those around totally dependent pupils are much more important than those surrounding other pupils. Their constant care requirements combined with communication difficulties mean that they are completely dependent on and constantly affected by the attitudes and values of those around them. They are unable, as most of us would do when faced with an attitude we did not share, to argue a point of view or remove themselves from the situation.

For each individual, the influences of home and school will be the most important, but the attitudes and values of parents and teachers cannot be considered in isolation, since they themselves will be affected by wider influences within society.

Attitudes and values are items not easy to quantify, and are shaped throughout life by the interaction of various spheres of influence on us all. Parental attitudes towards the education of their children are influenced by a great many factors, only one of which will be that their child has Rett Syndrome. Teachers of girls with Rett Syndrome will have differing attitudes towards teaching the girls. Their teaching experiences will be different and their attitudes towards the education of children with profound and multiple learning difficulties will similarly vary enormously.

Attitudes of society

Prior to 1970, children with profound learning difficulties were considered 'ineducable'. Special schools are now seen as an integral part of the education world as a whole. The fact that it was only just over twenty five years ago that these children were excluded from education altogether, illustrates how far attitudes have changed in this relatively short period of time.

Wolfensberger researched the attitudes of society towards those with learning difficulties, describing in 1969 the conflicting roles assigned by society to people with a learning disability, reported in Wood and Shears (1986) as:

1. The intended benign role – the person is seen as totally dependent, a 'poor innocent', seeking compassion and tolerance for her disability.
2. The malign role – when hostile and devaluing attitudes are held towards the disability and its harmful effects on others.
3. The actual benign role – when the disability is neither emphasised nor denied and opportunities are made for development of an individual's abilities.

It was argued by Wood and Shears that the interaction of these three assigned roles led to the development of a system that segregated people with learning disabilities, which in turn fostered the development of a 'them and us' attitude, mental handicap being seen as a 'problem' in the eyes of the general public, and a 'case for treatment' in the eyes of professionals.

Wolfensberger reported in 1994 on the further growth of a segregated system in a society with modernistic values. Materialism and the lack of spiritual depth in life, selfishness and sensualism meant that only those things that are of benefit to others, or were not draining on resources, were valued.

As regards mentally defective people specifically, they are defective bodies as viewed from a modernistic perspective. They are also seen as less able to obtain experience, enjoy or appreciate the pleasures of life. Some are offensive in appearance or behaviour. They are often viewed as obstacles to others. They are expensive consumers of resources, and in turn contribute little to the material prosperity of others.

(Wolfensberger 1994)

This somewhat frightening view was then contrasted with what Wolfensberger saw as a 'Message of Life'.

The creation of a new human being is a momentous – one could say miraculous – event of wondrous magnitude, regardless of the circumstances that surround it. From its very first beginning, each and every human being is of intrinsic, absolute, indivisible value. This implies that human dignity is derived by the mere existence of a human being, and is so neither earned by the individual, nor bestowed upon the person by other humans.

(Wolfensberger 1994)

Wolfensberger's analyses illustrated the conflicting views within society towards people with a learning disability. There is no doubt that the views prevalent within society will influence all those directly involved in the education of girls with Rett Syndrome, and affect their attitudes towards the work.

Attitudes of government

Over the last ten years, the education system in the UK has seen many changes. The Education Reform Act of 1988, the introduction of Local Management of Schools, including special schools, along with the introduction of a National Curriculum, have meant great changes in the schooling of children with special needs.

The term 'special needs' was introduced in the Warnock Report (1978) and enshrined in law by the 1981 Education Act, which revolutionised the education of children experiencing difficulties. Needs were identified in a legal document, a 'Statement of Educational Needs', with provision being made and resources identified to meet these needs.

The Warnock Report and the ensuing 1981 Education Act meant that children with special needs became a recognised part of the education system, working to the same aims. The creation of a 'Statement of Special Educational Needs', based on detailed individual assessment, provided the tools for the child to begin an individual path to attainment (Wood and Shears 1986). The procedures involved in drawing up Statements and their Annual Reviews was further refined by the Code of Practice (1994).

61

The importance of Statements and Annual Reviews is further described in the Specific Strategies section of this book.

The opening statement in *Curriculum Guidance 9 The National Curriculum and Pupils with Severe Learning Difficulties*, expresses the entitlement of all children:

> The Education Reform Act 1988 affirms that every pupil registered in maintained schools, including special schools, is entitled to a balanced and broadly based Curriculum.
>
> (National Curriculum Council 1992)

The nature of the curriculum itself is discussed elsewhere. What is of relevance here is the attitude of all-inclusiveness expressed by the government. This is further emphasised in the government publication for parents, *Special Educational Needs – A guide for parents*, published by the DFE following the introduction of the Code of Practice in 1994.

Madden (1995) argued that it made 'political sense' for government to work together with the parents of people with learning disabilities – parents being the main service providers, without whom services, especially for adults, would collapse.

The media

Brudenell (1986) lamented the lack of positive media coverage for those with severe learning difficulties, which, it was felt, led to their increasing isolation. The press often reported the negative aspect, 'that of horror stories and inquiries', but rarely the other side. She put forward the view that practitioners should 'jump up and down and shout' about the achievements of people with severe difficulties, and share expertise widely.

There is no doubt that media coverage can challenge views and provoke public and political opinion. The British Council of Organisations of Disabled People (BCODP 1995) tackled the negative images in the media of disabled people, and had a direct effect on television programme makers. Organisations such as The Centre for Studies on Integration have published widely, promoting the integration of children with special needs of all kinds (Allen 1987; Shaw 1990). Integration issues have been highlighted by the media, e.g. when parents wish their children with special needs to be educated in mainstream rather than special schools (Whitehead 1997).

The media image of children with profound learning difficulties plays an important part in the formation of current attitudes. Some disabled people are themselves able to directly campaign and work to change attitudes and stereotypical portrayals of disablement. For those with Rett Syndrome this can never be possible, and so it falls to support groups and parent organisations to work to overcome prejudice and effect a positive change in attitudes. However, it must not be overlooked that the energy of such people is limited by the very nature of their exhausting role caring for their disabled child.

The aims of education for pupils with profound and multiple learning difficulties

Ware (1994) expressed the aims of educating children with profound learning difficulties as 'enabling the child to participate in those experiences which are uniquely human'. The main aims of their education being enculturation, membership of the community and relationships with other humans. These aims would be further broken down to provide individual objectives. Ware recognised that for children who have profound and multiple difficulties, access to essential human experiences is limited by their disability and saw the role of education to increase their human experiences.

To define and interpret experiences that can be described as uniquely human is a challenging exercise. Trying then to see the world through the eyes of the profoundly disabled person, denied these experiences, is impossible. Wood and Shears (1986) pointed out that it is impossible for others to know how it feels to have profound and multiple difficulties such as Rett Syndrome, but attempts must be made in order that the educator can build respect for and accept the child as a valuable human being.

Labelling and diagnosis

Wood and Shears pointed out that the terms used to describe people with learning difficulties during this century have concentrated on the negative

63

aspects of the condition, which conjured up negative images. Although terms such as 'mentally subnormal' or 'simple' are not used nowadays, their replacements reinforced negative images by focusing on what is different about the person. Terms such as 'severe learning difficulties' and 'mental age', they said, detracted from the humanity of that person and encouraged a 'them and us' attitude.

BCODP (1995) described the 'Medical Model of Disability', which focused on the 'problems' experienced by disabled people. They suggested that it is not the actual impairments affecting people that 'disable' them, but the barriers and attitudes that divide them from the rest of society. They presented a 'Social Model of Disability' where, if these barriers were removed through anti-discrimination legislation, disability would not exist and disabled people would have the opportunity to achieve full equality.

When a child is diagnosed as suffering from a particular condition, there is a danger that the diagnosis can become a label. A danger of the labelling process is that the label becomes over-generalised, and places the emphasis on the handicap rather than on the person involved. This, Wood and Shears argued, perpetuates the negative attitudes to learning disabilities, since, if the labelling name itself has negative connotations, the negative feelings are transferred through the label to the person.

Brudenell (1986) discussed the possible consequences of a person becoming 'stuck' with a label. Labels and jargon were seen as empowering the user, enabling some professionals to baffle and impress. Labels were also seen as 'pegs on which to hang excuses for occurrences in which there is a need to apportion blame'.

Diagnosis is very important for the child and family. Brudenell (1986) noted the importance of specific information so that specialist equipment and help can be made available at the earliest possible opportunity to all involved in the care of the child.

Houghton (1994) found that diagnosis gave time for the family of the child with Rett Syndrome and services to work together to plan her future at every stage, to set in place coping strategies. It also gives a chance for parents to consider genetic counselling so as to be aware of the risks of having another child with similar difficulties (Pueschel 1988).

A diagnosis is particularly important in a condition such as Rett Syndrome, where the child's developmental pattern changes dramatically. An apparently 'normal' first 12 months, followed by a sudden regression, leads understandably to overwhelming confusion for parents and family. Diagnosis of this condition has only been available since 1983, and parents' feelings before diagnosis were described by Field (1990):

> Every Rett girl and her family before this date went through grotesque and seemingly inexplicable events which neither they nor the professionals could understand or predict.
> (Field 1990)

A diagnosis, even though it will be very painful in the case of a child with Rett Syndrome, gives the family a reason for what has happened, something to tell those who ask about her (Pueschel 1988). Information available at diagnosis should give parents some understanding of the condition, so events are no longer inexplicable. The family may have the opportunity to find out more about the condition, and join with others for mutual support if they wish to.

Diagnosis can give the family a realistic idea of their child's future. It was recognised that this will be very painful, remembering that with Rett Syndrome parents are usually assuming for her first 12 months that all is well with their daughter. Houghton (1994) described the very great shock and sense of loss parents faced when they realised the long-term nature of their daughters' condition.

The attitudes of schools

Johnson (1986 in Coupe and Porter) stated that special school staff must be very clear in their aims for the children in their care, and that these must be imparted through detailed information available whenever a decision is to be made about the child's education. It was acknowledged that for children with severe learning difficulties much of the evidence necessary to make decisions about the child's education will come from the feelings of the staff themselves. This was further emphasised by Brudenell.

> We will be ineffective in our work if we ignore what is going on within ourselves. But having insight into what we feel will make our work much easier – not physically but psychologically. If we can be at peace then this is something we can easily transfer to those in our care.
> (Brudenell 1986)

65

In a situation where learning may not be obvious due to the difficulties of the children, it is very important that staff work together and support each other, in order to recognise the achievement of individual children (Johnson 1986 in Coupe and Porter) A system that encouraged mutual support within the complex professional school structure was suggested, to foster positive attitudes towards the work.

It was recognised that, when working with children with severe learning difficulties, a balance has to be found by every individual between 'clinical over-detachment and over-emotional pity'. Johnson went on to explain that the key to this balance is respect. Professionals, it was suggested, need 'respect both for their pupils and their right to an individual human life; and respect for themselves as compassionate, competent professionals'.

The teachers

The most important person to the pupil with Rett Syndrome and her parents will usually be the class teacher. When teaching a child with multiple difficulties, the teacher needs to take on the role of a professional team member among those involved in helping the child. Such teachers will need to organise the work of others, such as support assistants and volunteers (Evans and Ware 1987).

Wood and Shears (1986) suggested that teachers of children with severe learning difficulties should examine their own assumptions and beliefs, and look at how these relate to their actions. If it is accepted that children with severe learning difficulties are individuals with the same basic rights as other people, then it is their right that their needs are fulfilled, the relationship between child and teacher requiring trust, autonomy and initiative. In order to accomplish this a recognition by staff that there is equality in relationships is vital. Recognising that the children have valid contributions to make, and respecting their wishes wherever possible, leads to acceptance of the child.

This acceptance has to be for the 'whole' child, and not for a collection of attributes. Teachers must, when working with children with profound and multiple difficulties, 'get beyond the casing that is their body, and somehow reach to their mind' (Brudenell 1986).

It has been emphasised that attitudes of teachers and all working with these children need to be flexible, with the knowledge that what works for one child will not necessarily work for another. Brudenell saw this as finding the 'key' for each individual that will open the door to progress. Teachers need to share their knowledge with the other professionals involved with the child in order that all may work together to maximise the child's progress.

An important part of the teacher's role is to foster good relations with the parents of the children in the class, and the difficulties this can present must not be underestimated. It is the parents that have responsibility for the child for the largest amount of time, and will have definite ideas as to how best to deal with the child and their difficulties. Johnson (1986 in Coupe and Porter) advocated that the teacher find out what sort of an individual the parents want as their son or daughter, and take careful note. Wadlow (1992 in Vulliamy and Webb) however reported that special schools did not provide time for teachers to meet with parents, and staff were not provided with the counselling skills that may be necessary.

The attitudes of schools towards parents

In all educational settings it is considered 'good practice' to foster and develop good relationships with the parents of the pupils. The introduction of the notion of 'Parents as Partners' re-emphasised this as government policy in the implementation of the National Curriculum (NCC 9:1992). The reasons for the particular importance of this partnership for children with severe learning difficulties were outlined by Helen McConachie (1986 in Coupe and Porter) and are summarised below:

- Parents are already the greatest influence on their children, their natural teachers. A partnership between school and home can build on this.
- The partnership between home and school can foster parents' confidence in their handling of the difficulties of their child.
- A partnership enables the working together of home and school in the priority areas of the child's curriculum.
- Children with severe learning difficulties require much structure in order to achieve their goals. A partnership enables consistency to develop, so parents are able to carry on the learning program at home.

How schools develop this partnership varies widely, as does the nature of the parental involvement itself. Adelman (1994) devised a model describing the levels and types of home involvement at school as being part of a continuum, where a parent contributing to the child's diary may be at one end, and parental involvement in LEA policy decision-making at the other.

Attitudes of parents

Beresford (1994) detailed many aspects of the lives of parents of severely disabled children. It was clear that the parents all wished to give their children the very best chances in life, their aspirations naturally reflecting the severity of the disabilities their child experienced. However, it was noted that many felt their aspirations were not matched by the provision of services, and so they began sometimes lengthy disputes with their LEA's.

This situation, Beresford noted, could also occur when cuts in provision affected children, an identified source of great stress to parents. Some parents, when not satisfied with what their child was offered, entered into costly and time-consuming private programmes of intensive treatment in order to fulfil a need to do everything possible to help their child, and to compensate for what they saw as inadequate provision.

Times of change for the child or parents were identified as a source of great anxiety to the family. Beresford described the 'fragile state in which many of these families exist'. An example was given of a family attending a workshop where they learnt more about their child's condition and needs, which led to dissatisfaction with the child's education. This had a 'ripple effect' on the whole family, as they considered private provision involving financial difficulties, moving house, battling with the authorities, all disturbing the state of equilibrium the family had worked hard to establish.

One attitude to education expressed by parents, and noted by Beresford, was that school provided a legitimate, safe form of respite care. Parents, faced with the 24 hour demands of a child with severe learning difficulties, expressed relief at being able to enjoy such pleasures as a trip to the shops unencumbered by a wheelchair, or a child with behavioural difficulties.

Some parents in the study readily accepted and benefited from professional assistance in such areas as toilet training, with which they were becoming increasingly frustrated at home. Others found school a help in providing regular activity for the child, which they saw as assisting in the regulation of sleep patterns and bed times.

Some welcomed the professional emotional support given by the school, in that they felt that they were no longer alone in coping with their child's problems, with advice and expert help on hand from someone who had got to know the child well. Wadlow (1992) described parents as feeling that school was 'one of the few places where staff listened to them and tried to understand their circumstances'.

Working together towards common goals was highlighted as an area in which parents felt a great sense of support. Home learning schemes, such as Portage, were mentioned as being supportive, helping parents learn how best to help their child in the early days.

Great pleasure was expressed by parents at sharing their child's progress in a school culture that celebrates the child's individual achievements.

A successful 'partnership with parents' apparently requires that a balance must be found between the parents and the professionals involved:

> Effective partnership within the education system will depend on honesty, respect and realistic expectations which recognise both the potential and limitations of parental involvement. Many parents need time and counselling in order to become agents rather than clients. Partnership is thus a continuous process which can adapt – and be adapted – for the mutual benefit of parents, children and professionals.
>
> (Russell, 1986 in Coupe and Porter)

Madden (1995) attributed changes in attitudes towards people with learning difficulties over the years to parents working in partnership with professionals influencing service development. Components for successful partnerships were identified as:

- positive attitudes of professionals towards parents;
- a willingness to work together;
- coherence of service providers;
- the development of parent empowerment systems;
- the encouragement of parents as agents of change.

Investigating attitudes and values of teachers and parents in the education of girls with Rett Syndrome

The teachers

The attitudes expressed by teachers towards working with pupils with Rett Syndrome were overwhelmingly positive. The girls appeared to be very popular with staff in all the schools visited, and were described in affectionate and loving terms. 'H--- is a very beautiful four year old girl. She has big bright eyes and a heart-warming smile.'

The positive attitudes expressed by virtually all teachers of girls with Rett Syndrome were extremely encouraging in that it provides evidence of a body of professionals dedicated to improving the educational opportunities of their pupils. The respect shown and dignity accorded them was obvious in many ways, such as the way in which they talked to the children or young adults.

Respect

An attitude of respect towards the girls was also evident in observations. One clear example of this was a class visited in a residential school where six students with Rett Syndrome had been placed. The teacher of the class insisted that all who came into contact with the teenagers referred to them as ladies rather than children and her respect for them was obvious. The respect shown and dignity accorded to the children was noted in many classes, especially where the pupils were older.

Apprehension

This was clearly explained to the researchers at an interview with six teachers at a mainstream middle school where two pupils with Rett Syndrome had recently begun attending. The initial fears felt by one teacher were honestly and vividly described; how he thought that he would find the children hard to look at; how he worried about the other pupils and their reaction to them; whether he could cope with their frailty and how the students themselves would fit into school life.

However, two months on, he felt differently, having got to know the students as individuals. All the staff were extremely positive, both about how their own attitudes to disability had changed, and how beneficial it was to all to have the students at school along with their peers.

The initial apprehension described by staff within a mainstream school was also evident among staff in special schools. Some teachers were concerned that they had such little information about the specific needs that accompany Rett Syndrome and some had heard the word 'regression' and thought, wrongly, that things could only get worse for their pupil. Once again, the apprehension was dispelled as the teachers got to know the girl and learnt more about the condition.

Apparent confidence in teachers did not appear to lead to complacency. Confidence appeared to grow along with the realisation that teaching a pupil with Rett Syndrome will be an on-going challenge, staff needing to become adaptable to the individuals' good and bad times.

Integration

The issue of children with such profound difficulties receiving their education at mainstream schools is not addressed in this book. However, it appears that attitudes towards such integration vary enormously among both professionals and parents.

During the course of this research it has become clear that it is, above all, the quality of the education that the girl with Rett Syndrome experiences that is all-important, before the where and who with. Strong views were expressed by proponents of both segregated and integrated education, by both teachers and parents. One view was clearly expressed by the Superintendent of Education of a School Board in Canada where all children were educated together. He explained his belief that everyone has a contribution to make, a part to play in society. Some build houses, some work computers, some grow food – all have a role. The role of those with profound disabilities is that of making the rest of us into better people.

Enquiring staff

The nature of their disabilities means that these pupils are unable to affect their environment unaided, being dependent on others to discover their strengths and preferences. This will require time, knowledge of the condition and detailed knowledge of the child. As one perceptive teacher responded 'one of the most challenging aspects of teaching a girl with Rett Syndrome, is asking the right questions, plumbing the depths'.

Nearly all the teachers were very eager to find out as much as possible about the nature of Rett Syndrome itself, and the particular difficulties faced by their pupil. Teachers who questioned, constantly enquiring into her individual needs, had built up detailed knowledge of the girl herself and formed close relationships with her parents. Armed with detailed knowledge of her individual needs, teachers sought long and hard to discover individual and often ingenious ways of teaching the particular girl they were working with. Equipment to stimulate activities was sought from far and wide and individually adapted to suit. Much was home-made.

Some teachers puzzled over questions such as 'How much does she retain from before her period of rapid skill loss?' and 'How much has she learnt since two and a half years of age?'

Teachers confident in their work appeared to employ every means at their disposal to learn more about the student, increasing awareness of her special needs, often involving close contact with other professionals. Teachers appeared then to add their own detailed observations and became able to pin-point reactions to certain stimuli. The use of video in classrooms aided some teachers, allowing close study of all reactions. Thus teachers employed flexible approaches, based on their study of the child, learning from her.

Intuition

Teachers used skills of intuition and careful observation coupled with their knowledge of the child to develop and plan teaching. 'I feel that she could learn much through the use of music and drama, where she really seems to "come alive" and indicates that she has a lot to offer by making intense eye contact, increasing movements and vocalisation.'

It was evident that teachers used intuition and careful observation to analyse the students' particular difficulties. Added to their own observational skills, some teachers utilised technology to aid analysis of the individual's difficulties – for example, video recording allowed teachers to identify many reactions that were not immediately obvious.

Intuition plays a large part for teachers in their work with pupils with Rett Syndrome. They appeared to rely on their own judgement of the girls potential and work towards it.

Frustration

Frustration was occasionally expressed by teachers at specific aspects of the pupil's behaviour. It was expressed many times that teachers felt that the girls knew far more than they showed. Assessments were often cited in this connection since teachers felt that the low scores attributed in no way reflected the child's abilities. When a student's assessed mental age was mentioned, it was nearly always followed by a qualifying statement, along the lines of 'It doesn't do her justice'.

Inconsistency on a daily basis was a source of frustration for some teachers. Often, a success noted one day was unobtainable the next. It was reported that teaching a girl with Rett Syndrome can sometimes be like 'stabbing around in the dark'. This could sometimes be attributed to her 'moods', but often there was no apparent reason for the inconsistency. Reactions could vary from hour to hour, and success achieved needed to be recorded instantly, as it might not be repeated for days.

All teachers seemed to experience times of frustration, perhaps at the student's apparent lack of interest or response. Sometimes they were concerned at their own inexperience and lack of knowledge, while at other times they felt that the girl was not indicating her true abilities and knew much more than she was capable of demonstrating.

It appears that a team approach, where different staff are working with the child in an open, mutually supportive way can combat this frustration. In a team that celebrates successes and analyses failures, a temporary lack of confidence can quickly be restored and another idea tried or another avenue explored. Such a team of people would ideally include the physiotherapists and any other therapists that worked with the child. Evidence of this was unfortunately not commonly found. Some teachers seemed to see therapy as separate, the therapists often seen as fleeting visitors to the classroom. Where therapists formed a part of the teaching team, therapy was more likely to be undertaken as a part of the child's curriculum in a creative way.

The parents

Following the examination of the teachers' attitudes, a separate small-scale study was carried out to investigate the attitudes of parents towards the education of their daughters with Rett Syndrome. Responses were received from the parents of 26 girls aged from 3 years to 17 years in the UK. These girls are educated in a variety of settings, the overwhelming majority of which are SLD schools.

For most parents, the entry of their daughter will be their first introduction to a special school environment. All will have had experience of education themselves which will affect their expectations of the school, and their views on their daughters' schooling. In the survey half the parents reported positive opinions about their own education, and a small number indicated very negative feelings.

Positive attitudes

It was clear from the data that the parents involved were nearly all very positive about the education of their daughters. This is summed up by one parent: 'school is an outlet for her, and a well-earned respite for me. She enjoys it so much, and it makes me so happy to see her smile and be content with the people she knows around her that love and care for her.' On the whole parents held overwhelmingly positive views towards schools for their daughters with Rett Syndrome. It was clear that they not only appeared satisfied with the service offered, but were often delighted with certain aspects of it.

Attitudes towards staff

The most appreciated aspect of schools were the staff. Many parents felt strongly that the staff at their daughter's school cared deeply about her. One parent wrote that she liked the 'caring staff with a good attitude to handicap'. Another noted the staff's attitude to her daughter in that they showed 'affection and sincerity' when working with her. Another felt that the staff's attitude was 'exemplified by the respect shown to the children and parents, and the loving care she receives from staff.'

The fact that the staff wanted to get to know the girl was also popular, described by one parent as 'the teachers' willingness to learn about my daughter'. Parents also liked the way in which the staff were flexible in their dealings with individuals, and made efforts to meet each girl's particular needs. One parent said, 'They recognise R's needs, having adapted the school day to her'. The staff's willingness to persevere with the child was liked – 'they never give up on her or her abilities'.

Quality teaching

Many of the parents felt that their daughter's school offered high quality teaching with clear progress being observed – 'her progress since starting school is most noticeable'. Planned and regularly reviewed individual programmes were clearly approved of, along with innovation, some staff being seen as 'courageous enough to try appropriate new ideas'.

Evidence of progress in their daughters was noted by parents, and it is clear that many felt involved in the programme planning, and so could share successes. Many parents welcomed this involvement, realising the vital part played by the information they give about their daughter. This partnership between home and school, once formed, appeared to further contribute to the development of positive attitudes towards the school. The professional help offered by staff was seen to benefit not only the child's time at school, but the whole of her life.

Therapy

For many girls with Rett Syndrome, regular physiotherapy is very important to maintain their physical well-being. Many parents were very positive about their daughters receiving physiotherapy at school, where the therapists were seen as being to hand. Their involvement in the girl's therapy was very important to several parents, and, for some, access to physiotherapy was the best thing about their daughter's school.

However, it was also clear that many of the parents felt that their daughters did not get enough therapy, with concern being expressed over the apparently decreasing services available. A large proportion of the parents felt their daughters would benefit from music therapy, and activities such as horse riding, which were currently unavailable to them. Under-funding was a concern for many of the parents, especially in terms of staffing. Several parents felt that their daughter would benefit from more individual assistance.

Atmosphere

'Atmosphere' was mentioned as something parents particularly liked about their daughters' schools. This was described in various ways as 'homely', 'caring', 'happy', 'relaxed', 'stimulating' and 'open'. It would be interesting to research which adjectives parents of typical children in a mainstream school offered to describe what they liked about the atmosphere at their children's schools. This could possibly indicate similarities and differences in attitudes towards mainstream and special education.

Facilities

Good facilities in a school were recognised, as was a willingness on the school's part to be inventive in a time of cuts. Space and size of the school were of concern to some parents for a variety of reasons. Facilities at a few schools were disliked, one parent describing 'outdated and decrepit buildings'. Facilities were mentioned comparatively little, and appeared not to figure highly in the parents' assessment of a school.

Communications

The school and teachers' communications with parents were felt to be very important. Parents appreciated consultation about their child's programmes, and enjoyed regular contact with the school. Some parents also felt that the school offered the family support as well as the girl with Rett Syndrome. 'They try to cater for everyone's needs, parents as well.'

The quality of the relationship that is built up with the family appeared to be dependent upon the quality of communication between home and school. Schools that had developed effective systems of communicating with parents on a personal, even daily level, were seen by parents in a positive light.

The value of education to the parents of girls with Rett Syndrome

Parents were asked what they considered to be the most valuable things education gave to their daughter with Rett Syndrome. Their expressed preferences are listed and discussed below.

Social contact

The contact the child had with other children was the most important aspect of her education to the parents involved in the study. 'An opportunity to mix with and enjoy her peers.' Some saw mixing with others as an important part of her development, in that she was 'having to communicate with other people'.

For children who require every social contact to be arranged for them, school offers a supported friendship group, with a variety of opportunities to experience different social settings. The trip to town as a teenager was never the same with parents as with a group of peers. These girls may enjoy opportunities to giggle together while trying the demonstration products at the beauty stands, or sharing a coffee time noisily as a group in a café.

Opportunities

A large number of the parents felt that education extended their child's opportunities and her knowledge. Learning about the world, and developing awareness and interest in it were seen as important. One parent wrote that she felt that education gave her daughter 'a sense of the world, and a sense of herself in the world'.

Schools offer a variety of learning experiences that are part of the curriculum yet take place outside school. Visits to art galleries, theatres and even residential visits to other parts of the country provide opportunities for the student to widen her experience and knowledge.

Stimulation

Stimulation and 'keeping the girl motivated' were highlighted by some parents as important aspects of their daughters' education. 'Keeping up the struggle' was how one parent described it! Another said that their daughter received 'encouragement to persevere, every little achievement bringing praise and appreciation of how much she has achieved'.

Independence

For some parents, developing independence was important. It was felt that education 'helped her grow up' and that it encouraged her in 'learning about herself'. It was also pointed out that it gave her time, spent away from the family, 'being taken seriously, a person in her own right'.

Therapy

A small number of parents thought that the most important thing education gave their daughter was access to therapy. Regular physiotherapy was seen as particularly important to maintain as much mobility as possible. The therapists are employed by the local health authority rather than the education authority who employ most staff at the school, a situation which can create division, as staff are responsible to different managers with differing agendas and budgets. This can work directly against the development of multi-professional teams that include teachers and therapists.

The parents wanted therapy to take place in school rather than a hospital or medical centre. However if therapy is to become a part of the girl's individual curriculum, then teachers and therapists need to work closely together to make it an integral part of her personal timetable.

Conclusions

There are many influences on society's attitude towards special education. Initially these will be formed from the history and traditions of the culture, and embrace the way in which children with disabilities are viewed. Any change in attitudes will be slow and take many years to evolve.

Successfully meeting the needs of pupils with Rett Syndrome will require an increasing knowledge and understanding of the condition, along with further research into their wide-ranging needs. Policy and resourcing decisions that affect the education of girls with Rett Syndrome can only be made with a knowledge of the condition and its devastating effects on the individual and her family.

The issue of integration has been raised in many forums over the last fifteen years. However, it is the experience of the researchers that there remains a wide diversity of attitudes towards the integration of girls with Rett Syndrome, among both teachers and parents. Those committed to integration, and involved in successful projects, express very positive committed views, sometimes admitting to initial reluctance. There are also those who are as firmly committed to segregation. This debate goes on, its very existence raising awareness of the difficulties faced by teachers and parents in devising suitable educational programmes for children with Rett Syndrome.

It appears, however, that it is the quality of the education that is more important than its location. Good practice offering the girl with Rett Syndrome an education of high quality was found in a wide variety of settings.

There is a clear need for mutual awareness between parents and teachers. Teachers need to be aware of parental concerns, and parents need to be aware that their child is part of a group at school. Teachers can bring their professional skills and experience to a partnership with parents, who have detailed knowledge of the child. This partnership must be balanced, each side respecting and listening to the other's point of view.

Forming a balanced partnership with parents can be one of the most challenging aspects of the teachers role, especially in the special school. The children may travel quite a distance to the school, and so the parent may not feel she knows anyone at the school. Teachers need to welcome parents, and, from the evidence gathered in this small scale study, it seems that they do, and that their efforts are much appreciated by the parents who appeared to admire their flexibility and perseverance.

One aspect of school parents expressed grave concerns about was the continuing reduction in funding in special schools, especially where staffing in their daughter's classroom was affected. Fears were expressed about the health and safety of their very vulnerable girls, especially in classes where other children's difficulties led to parents envisaging serious accidents occurring due to inadequate staffing. These concerns will be greater at times of change to a new class or school, but they appear increasingly to be a major source of worry and stress to parents.

Parents value education for their daughters with Rett Syndrome highly. In this study, it was seen as of particular value in meeting her social needs. In addition to this, parents valued the wide opportunities education offers – the stimulation, motivation and the chances it gives her for some small measure of independence.

Considering the attitudes and values of teachers and parents can provide a school with long-term goals. These are not specific to Rett Syndrome alone and can also be applied to other children who experience severe and profound and multiple learning difficulties. To change takes a long time, but it is vital to consider the attitudes of all involved in working with such children.

In working with the girl with Rett Syndrome, everyone is faced with a mystery in which sometimes all will seem fine, planning perfectly matching performance, and at other times achievements will appear minute or non-existent. Attitudes that offer respect and afford her dignity will illustrate the value put on her education, and so enhance the whole of her life.

Chapter 9

The curriculum

In Great Britain prior to 1971, pupils with severe and complex learning difficulties, as is evident in Rett Syndrome, were considered to be ineducable and did not receive education. Many were cared for in Junior Training Centres, in which the ethos emphasised personal care routines, 'keeping them happy', and offering respite to parents. 'This ethos is still evident in some schools today and has been used, in some instances, as a justification for rejecting the National Curriculum.' (Sebba *et al.* 1993)

In the early years of special education, the medical model prevailed. Pupils were described on the basis of what they could not do as a result of various syndromes, and any pupil with a particular diagnosis was assumed to have all the characteristics of that syndrome. Such preconceived notions of pupils' abilities can serve to justify their failure to learn, and so disable them further.

The 1970 Education Act (Handicapped Children) established the rights of pupils with severe and complex learning difficulties to enter the educational system. The Warnock Report on 'Handicapped Children and Young People' (DES 1978), which followed mounting pressures, enhanced the position of these pupils by stating that the goals of education were the same for all pupils. In relation to special education, the Department of Education and Science (1978) established that 'the purpose of education for all children is the same. But the help that individual children need in progressing towards them will be different.'

The 1981 Education Act indicated that, whereas some pupils will always have special educational needs, these will not remain static but will change as the pupil matures and develops. The Act recognised that appropriate curricular provision was dependent on the allocation of additional resources. The procedures of drawing up Statements of Special Educational Need and having an annual review system were devised to ensure that the necessary resources were available.

The whole curriculum

Prior to the introduction of the National Curriculum, there was an increasing understanding of what should constitute a curriculum for all pupils.

The Education Reform Act (1988) stated that every pupil was entitled to 'a broad, balanced, relevant and differentiated curriculum' which met his or her needs. 'That principle must be reflected in the curriculum of every pupil. It is not enough for such a curriculum to be offered by the school. It must be fully taken up by each individual pupil.' ('National Curriculum From Policy to Practice', DES 1989b)

'A Curriculum for All' (National Curriculum Council 1989a) developed these ideas, emphasising the need not only for access to a broad, balanced, relevant and differentiated curriculum, but also for progression and continuity within it.

The Curriculum from 5–16 (DES 1989a) identified the following essential areas of learning: aesthetic and creative, human and social, linguistic and literary, mathematical, moral, physical, scientific, spiritual and technological. 'Each . . . [area] . . . should be represented in one form or another in the curriculum throughout the period of compulsory schooling'. (DES 1989a)

Fagg *et al.* (1990) evaluated current legislation and guidance with respect to pupils with severe and complex learning difficulties. They defined the whole curriculum for such pupils as consisting of all the National Curriculum subjects: English, mathematics, science, technology, art, PE, music, history, geography, religious education and a modern foreign language for pupils aged 12 and over as well as other aspects considered vital by the school.

Ouvry (1991) defined the whole curriculum for pupils with profound and multiple learning difficulties as the National Curriculum, overlapping with a developmental curriculum and an additional curriculum as necessary, according to need.

A developmental curriculum will consist of those elements traditionally defined within a special school – the individual aims and objectives to meet the special educational needs for each pupil or group of pupils. The additional curriculum will consist of the therapies, special programmes and new approaches which contribute to 'the pattern of each pupil's educational experience'.

The 1993 Education Act required the Secretary of State to issue a Code of Practice giving practical guidance to Local Education Authorities and governing bodies of all schools in discharging their responsibilities towards all children with special educational needs. The Code of Practice also placed similar responsibilities on the health and social services.

The annual review of the statement achieved more significance following the Code of Practice, and the LEA has an increased responsibility to ensure that parents are fully involved, that all relevant professionals have the chance to contribute, that annual objectives are set and assessed each year and that the statement is amended if necessary. In practice, this responsibility is often delegated to the school.

Timetables

The breadth of need as defined in the child's statement of special educational needs should be evaluated within the Annual Review of the statement. Timetabling and resources must ensure that all pupils have equal opportunities to this breadth, whether incorporating the National Curriculum in its entirety, or appropriate alternatives. Fagg *et al.* (1990) considered that this balance could only be achieved if the development of the social, emotional, intellectual and physical attributes of the pupils are considered and given equal value.

There is, perhaps, a general assumption that timetables represent a picture of what is offered to the pupils. 'An analytical glance over a few timetables suggests that this is not the case.' (Sebba *et al.* 1993)

These authors considered that items on the timetable such as 'individual activities' or 'options' described teaching styles rather than curricular content. Similarly, 'soft play' or 'minibus' serve only as 'logistical signposts'. Timetables, then, may indicate the 'how' or 'where' rather than the 'what' of teaching. When analysing the timetables of pupils with Rett Syndrome, this particular point was well-illustrated and it was not always easy to determine curriculum priorities based on timetables alone.

Findings from observations and questionnaires

Separate subjects seldom appeared on the timetables seen within the study, or in individual plans. However, observed or reported activities have been listed that fall within the curriculum areas nationally prescribed within this country at present. In order to present the information, it is helpful to organise the presentation within the 'whole curriculum' as described by Ouvry earlier.

The National Curriculum

English

National Curriculum English incorporates speaking and listening; reading and writing. In practice, many schools for pupils with severe or profound learning difficulties would consider that the teaching of communication skills was appropriate work within part of the English curriculum. Data analysis revealed how teachers were ensuring that girls with Rett Syndrome had access to this area of the curriculum.

Of the 22 girls in the initial pilot study, the teachers of 21 identified communication as a curriculum priority. Communication in its broadest sense is the 'speaking and listening' for those with Rett Syndrome.

Girls with Rett Syndrome were communicating through: eye contact with a sustained gaze; showing consistent responses to likes / dislikes; vocalising to gain attention; expressing needs through body language; expressing moods through music and drama; communicating through interaction with others; eye gaze to objects; using objects of reference / environmental cues; eye pointing to photos, pictures and symbols; using simple gestures; sign language; using technological aids and, in a few cases vocalisations and speech.

The use of photos, pictures and symbols are accepted pre-reading skills, and used by many girls to represent, or communicate about, an object, a person or a thought by means of these visual images. Several teachers mentioned that pupils with Rett Syndrome enjoyed listening to stories or looking at books, photos or pictures. Many girls particularly liked looking at photos of themselves or their family, and showed recognition of such photos. One girl was learning to recognise 'her' belongings in school by means of an abstract shape (a red plastic cube) on the back of her chair, her coat peg, her drawer.

In almost all the classes visited, symbols were used in order to try and bring meaning to the girls' world, for example: symbol timetables, symbol labels, weather symbols etc. Many girls were using standardised picture symbols such as Makaton or Meyer Johnson. One girl recognised her name written on a card among other children's names.

The necessary fine motor skills and coordination required for writing are unlikely to be adequately developed in pupils with Rett Syndrome. However, many girls enjoyed finger painting or other tactile activities such as spreading shaving foam on a table top, or working with their hands in sand. Others were able to draw single strokes using a pen, crayon or paintbrush. For most, though, these early writing activities offer more in the way of sensory stimulation and exploration than a realistic progression towards writing.

One girl was able to eye-point from a choice of symbols in order for it to be stuck on and so 'write about' her work. Another girl, in a mainstream secondary school in the USA was reported to use her strong eye-gaze to indicate correct/incorrect spellings in her class's weekly test.

Mathematics
National Curriculum Mathematics incorporates: using and applying mathematics; number (and algebra for over 7s); shape, space and measures and handling data (for over 7s). Many perceptual tasks could be considered as early mathematics development.

Despite their limited hand function, most girls with Rett Syndrome can use their hands as 'tools' with which to undertake practical tasks – hitting, shaking, grasping and letting go. Materials with a strong sensory element – bright, eye-catching, noisy – were used successfully in many of the classes visited.

Many teachers of pupils with Rett Syndrome were working on stimulation of the senses in order to develop perceptual awareness and sensory motor skills. One teacher might favour working with tracking lights in the dark room, whilst another might use a joystick on a computer. Students with Rett Syndrome were observed working well with both these media.

As has been outlined earlier, all the girls could show, by their reactions, the sensations which they liked or disliked. Many girls had a repertoire of consistent behaviours (smiling, grimacing, moving towards or away) which served to indicate the choices they could make.

Many of the girls in the study showed evidence of being able to make predictions based on experience – like the girl who knew that if she rocked long enough the clock would fall to the floor and cause chaos! Other instances include the (many) girls who understood how to disrupt, and be removed from, a lesson which they did not enjoy; the girl who showed increasing excitement until her favourite page in the book was reached; the girl who stands and stares for minutes at a time into the cupboard, until a sympathetic adult realises she is waiting for the cassette player, stored there out of sight.

Almost all could, through their body language and behaviour, indicate 'again', 'more' and 'no more'. They could anticipate personal care routines too, and laugh uproariously when something went wrong!

Many girls were able to look at one object, and to choose one object from a choice of two or three: what to have for lunch; which colour paint to use; who to sit next to. One indicated very convincingly her understanding of 'more' and 'less' when she compared her pile of crisps to her neighbour's.

Some of the girls visited were working on matching in pairs – perhaps with pictures or symbols, or using a touchscreen.

Algebra can, arguably, be described as an understanding of pattern and sequence in order to make sense of the world. Many girls had developed a sound understanding of the patterns and sequences in their daily life – when their school bus was due; at the end of grandma's road; when she heard the clatter of lunchtime plates. Others could recognise rhythms in music, and beat on a drum to their favourite music.

Many girls were encouraged to explore shapes either through visual image or touch. Some of this work was undertaken in a 'white room', with a 'feely box', or with more conventional equipment.

Sensory work was used in many schools to offer the girls opportunities to develop their attention skills and visual or auditory tracking – above them, behind, moving across etc.

Several girls were able to select objects according to extreme differences (e.g. the big one, from a choice of two).

Science

National Curriculum Science incorporates: experimental and investigative science (exploring, observing, communicating and predicting); life processes and living things (using own ideas, developing a knowledge of the difference between things which are alive, and things which are not – humans as organisms); materials and their properties (grouping and changing materials) and physical processes (experiencing electricity, forces and motion, light and sound).

Throughout the many schools visited, girls with Rett Syndrome were encouraged to use their senses to explore and recognise similarities and differences between materials. A sensory approach to the curriculum was seen, by many teachers, to offer a 'core' science curriculum for pupils with profound and multiple learning difficulties. Thus, cookery experiences were chosen for their strong sensory element – perhaps cooking onions, which are hard, brown and cold before cooking and become soft and warm when cooked. In addition, it is difficult to be unaware of the smell of onions cooking! Science seemed to offer rich opportunities to touch, taste, smell and look, and consequently to interest and motivate.

All the girls could communicate their reactions to the various experiences, and communicate them to their teachers. Some could demonstrate surprise – a big laugh; or make predictions (doing something again that they enjoyed).

All the girls were able to recognise familiar people, and to respond to them by touching, looking, moving towards or away. A few could demonstrate knowledge of certain body parts in order to 'join in' – moving a hand or foot when encouraged, for example. Many were described as liking particular 'categories' of people – perhaps babies or, very commonly, men!

Tactile stimulation was used with many girls, and their responses noted and acted upon. Some disliked intensely being 'manipulated' to explore by touch. Others, however, were reported to respond well – perhaps to being cuddled, or touching something warm.

Many girls were being encouraged to explore materials with different properties. Responses were varied, according to each individual, but some were happy to feel sand, paint, hand cream etc.

A number of girls had developed preferences for certain toys or equipment according to their sensory properties – a pretty tune, a sparkly appearance, etc. Battery operated equipment, or toys with switches, offered play and learning opportunities for many pupils with Rett Syndrome. Some had access to well-equipped interactive sensory environments, whilst others had more modest resources. However, many girls enjoyed the 'low effort / big impact' effect of such technology.

Many responded well to everyday appliances and toys such as torches, clocks, musical toys and cassette players. Simple switches often offered the student a rare opportunity to control her environment.

For girls who had appropriate physical skills, swings and wheel toys were enjoyed. One young lady, in Canada, was very proficient indeed on a bike – with only a minimum of assistance. Girls generally had more success pushing large pieces of equipment (rollator, doll's pram) rather than smaller ones (cars, marbles).

Technology

Of the girls seen in the study, their contribution to technology lay in assisting to assemble objects (e.g. decorating a box). By necessity, this was often hand over hand. Usually she was offered some choice of colours/materials. Although their chances of participation were limited, most girls enjoyed the one-to-one needed to complete their work, and often seemed pleased with their results.

There are a number of skills and experiences which are basic within a design and technology curriculum such as communicating, choosing and manipulating materials which were pursued throughout the girls' education, even if not as part of the design and technology curriculum.

History

Throughout the visits to all the schools, only one identified history lesson was observed. A girl in an integrated secondary school in Canada worked, with an assistant, on weaving on a replica of an Iron-Age loom.

History has been defined as: 'the study of the past . . . in order to better understand the present' (Sebba 1994). In this context, girls were seen working on cause and effect, recording events through pictures or symbols and learning to appreciate the consequences of their actions. Similarly, photos and symbols were used to aid their understanding of 'what comes next' (e.g. a symbol timetable for the day), or 'when we did . . .' (e.g. a photo record book of a trip) which served to place her activities in a logical sequence or remind her of a recent event in the past.

Geography

Although not specifically called 'Geography' in any school, many girls were observed undertaking work which is clearly a part of the Geography curriculum. Often as part of a daily routine, they were shown symbols relating to weather conditions for that day, sometimes experiencing the elements directly first! Teaching through themes, or topics, offered many girls Geographical experiences – a visit to a farm, a trip to the beach, learning about homes or jobs – which served to bring breadth, experience and interest to their learning. 'Geography is about the relationship between people and places. It aims to help pupils make sense of their surroundings and develop an understanding about the interaction of people with the environment' (Sebba 1995).

Art

Most art work observed in the study involved an adult manipulating a girl's hands in order to produce work. This may be justified as 'art' in order that she may experience different media: the activity in itself has purpose. Pupils with Rett Syndrome may well find it impossible to use art as a means of representing their world, their lives or their feelings through drawings, paintings, sculpture and textiles. However, using these media offered them rich opportunities to explore surface texture, shape and form. Combining sensory activities in order to create an effect – temporary or permanent – seemed to offer the most useful access to art·for students with Rett Syndrome.

Piotrowski (in Harrison 1994) described art as 'visual literacy which she defined as 'recognising, describing and responding to our world and the forms of art using the language of art: line, tone, pattern, texture, colour, shape, form and space'. Access to a wide range of visual experiences can, thus, enrich the life of every child with Rett Syndrome.

Music

The study showed that one of the most common areas of the curriculum which the girl with Rett Syndrome could participate in and enjoy was music. They all demonstrated an awareness of sound, many of them had favourite types or individual pieces of music, and a significant number were observed actively participating in music sessions.

Teachers sought to develop rhythmic awareness in the girls through action songs, body movements to music and dance. Musical toys and equipment were reported to be highly motivating with many.

One music session observed involved seven girls with Rett Syndrome working with one teacher and several assistants. The girls' anticipation was electric, and each eagerly awaited her turn. Although their delayed response, and apraxia, was evident, they showed recognition of their names in song and were able to play percussion instruments such as drums, cymbals etc. in turn. One girl demonstrated her memory of being allowed to play the piano the previous week by sulking when there was no time the following week!

Music therapy offered a truly participative medium for girls with Rett Syndrome. What was also striking when a video camera was used to record a music therapy session, was one girl's delayed response and apraxia building up prior to her gathering her resources to overcome both in order to participate. This offered strong evidence of the powerful motivation music offered to pupils with Rett Syndrome.

Physical education

Physical education in England and Wales incorporates gymnastics, dance, games and, for pupils in Key Stage 2 and above (eight year olds onwards) swimming.

Movement usually comes spontaneously to children, combined with their desire to explore their environment in a variety of ways. Girls with Rett Syndrome, however, may have missed some, or even all, of these typical experiences. Many are completely dependent on other people, and the majority have an impaired ability to initiate, control or sustain their movement.

Gymnastics: Much of the work seen in this area involved the girl with Rett Syndrome in close physical contact with her teacher. This included:

- holding and rocking her – often to music and sometimes working with more independent peers;
- being moved across large items of gymnastic equipment – such as slides and physio balls;
- using large surfaces of the body for support;
- the use of adapted bikes and crawler boards to give a sense of movement.

Dance: Expressive movement can help to develop a child's ability to communicate and foster their expertise in self-expression and body language. For girls with Rett Syndrome, dance offered a good opportunity to link music with physiotherapy. Some teachers used gentle swaying, turning, rocking and enclosing movements – to music – providing security and confidence in being handled. Specific exercises combined with music were sometimes used to bend and stretch limbs appropriately. Several girls with Rett Syndrome were described as enjoying dancing to music at their own pace, and in their own style.

Games: The teaching of games offers the opportunity for girls to experience enjoyment and participation with others, and also to reinforce skills in a practical situation. Games usually concentrate on using the whole body, and are concerned with space, time and weight.

Given their difficulty in using their hands, the games observed involved individual practice with various types and sizes of ball, parachute games and games incorporated into Conductive Education groups, e.g. hitting skittles in turns within a circle group. Rhythmic intention, an essential element of conductive education, was found helpful for several pupils with Rett Syndrome. The use of rhymes and songs to emphasise movement seemed to help reinforce their intention of action.

Swimming: Most girls with Rett Syndrome swam in hydrotherapy pools. The use of a hydrotherapy pool for swimming, however, does not constitute 'therapy' although there are many common elements between the two.

In both cases, working in water offers the child with Rett Syndrome the chance to:

- have fun and enjoyment;
- improve and maintain muscle tone and promote motor fitness;
- promote her cardio-vascular fitness;
- perform movements otherwise impossible on 'dry land';
- improve her body awareness and knowledge of the relationship between body parts;
- increase her confidence and self-esteem.

In addition, hydrotherapy is carried out by a physiotherapist and involves patterns of movement adapted to water and more water-specific exercises. Hydrotherapy can be very successful in integrating therapeutic and recreational activities for those with Rett Syndrome.

In some schools, pools had been adapted to include lights and music, and so incorporate a further dimension to the sensory curriculum.

No girl with Rett Syndrome should ever be unattended in the water, irrespective of any buoyancy aids.

Information and communication technology

This can be described as: 'the use of tools as a means by which we present, store or process information' (Banes and Coles, 1995).

Information and communication technology (ICT) was used in a wide range of ways in many of the schools visited. Equipment which offered sensory stimulation was considered very valuable. Girls were observed operating simple switches in order to control bubble tubes, flashing lights, cassette players. Switches and joysticks could be manipulated by some girls to operate computer programmes, and others could use touch screens to achieve a similar effect. Mercury tilt switches had been tried with one girl in order to discourage hand movements. The switch operated a battery toy when the girl's hands and arms were down, and the toy 'cut out' if she lifted them to flap. ICT supported teaching and learning in a highly motivating context.

Music technology seemed to motivate many of the girls. Keyboards offer interesting opportunities for exploring music-making, whilst a sound beam, sensitive enough to be operated by the blink of an eye, gave access to music for those with greatly impaired physical skills.

ICT offered a range of ways of meeting the girls' needs: for example, one girl used a 'low tech' system of eye-pointing to symbols pasted on a board, whilst another used a more 'high tech' electronic communication aid (Introtalker). The use of switches to indicate choice was being developed in different ways in many schools. In general, the simplest tools were often the most effective, minimising the effort required for the girl to coordinate her hands and eyes or to carry out a movement. Many were reported as reacting to particular sounds – favourite music, the sound of the school bus. Computers were also used by some, operated by a touch screen or a joystick.

Girls with Rett Syndrome responded to a range of means of storing information. Many used pictures or photos which they enjoyed looking at, could point to in various ways, or used to indicate decisions and choices. Videotape of themselves and their friends or family were also reported as successful with some girls. One girl chose from a range of symbols in order to label her work. One pupil understood that her actions on a joystick created visual and auditory feedback via the computer monitor.

Some girls were seen to be using simple switches, through an interface box, to control battery and mains toys and equipment, for example, lights, battery toys, cassette players and radios, bubble tubes in Snoezelen rooms etc. Soundbeam was described by one teacher as offering her pupil with Rett Syndrome the opportunity to make sounds and music. Another girl was exploring the means of operating her wheelchair by a kick of the foot.

Information and communication technology undoubtedly offers girls with Rett Syndrome significant opportunities to access the whole curriculum. ICT is an integral part of our everyday experience, and should also be an integral part of work and leisure opportunities for those with Rett Syndrome.

Religious education

Legally, every school in England and Wales must offer religious education to all pupils throughout their school career, unless parents request otherwise. Religious education is defined as a curriculum which: 'promotes the spiritual, moral, cultural, mental and physical development of pupils at the school and . . . prepares such pupils for the opportunities, responsibilities and experience of adult life.' (Education Reform Act, 1988. 1.2b)

The development of the senses of taste, smell, sound, vision, touch and bodily experience are the first steps in learning. Longhorn suggested that religious education offered a new sense 'in which to enhance and deepen sensory learning'. She described this as the 'numinous sense' and suggested that it incorporated:

- a sense of mystery, awe, wonder and attraction;
- feelings beyond understanding;
- a non-rational element of religious experience;
- a sense of communion with nature, divinity or the unknown.

(Longhorn, 1993)

Several examples of what Longhorn described as the numinous sense were reported in girls with Rett Syndrome. Several, for example, would cry when listening to a particular piece of music. Others had exhibited deep sadness in appropriate situations – picking up on emotions when a close relative had died, for example. Others were reported as becoming exhilarated by situations, music, experiences and places. Possibilities within topics provided further opportunities for girls with Rett Syndrome to participate in religious education. However, most schools relied on religious education being implicit within the whole curriculum rather than planning explicit schemes of work.

In one school, where those with Rett Syndrome were fully integrated within a mainstream school, religious education was one subject where they participated alongside their peers without differentiation.

The developmental curriculum

The developmental curriculum refers to those subjects and approaches traditionally offered within a 'special' school. Historically, many schools for children with severe or profound learning difficulties invested great time and effort in devising developmentally-based curriculum objectives based on 'normal' milestones. However, during more recent years a more holistic approach to children's learning has evolved, incorporating the breadth required of a modern curriculum combined with specialist approaches to teaching and learning where appropriate.

The Department of Education and Science and Welsh Office (1984b) described a developmental curriculum as 'covering selected and sharply focused educational, social and other experiences with precisely defined objectives and designed to encourage a measure of personal autonomy.'

The following examples of specialist provision was observed in the education of girls with Rett Syndrome:

Behaviour modification
Behaviour modification is a type of therapy that relies on operant conditioning (using a controlled and planned programme of reinforcement) to change behaviour. Once widely used with pupils with severe learning difficulties, this technique became outmoded in more recent years, as this approach offered little scope for personal autonomy or choice for the pupil. Certain techniques remain as useful tools for the special educator, but this approach is now seldom used as a method of defining curriculum content.

One girl was placed within a class of pupils with severe learning difficulties who also displayed challenging behaviours, and in which behaviour modification was employed as an approach to teaching and learning.

The behavioural approach was not being used rigidly with this pupil who was a member of the class for mainly pragmatic reasons, as it was felt that 'she does not fit in any other class'. This teacher was well-placed to

93

evaluate behaviour modification as an approach to teaching a girl with Rett Syndrome and felt it was not effective. She felt that the 'barriers to learning' were beyond the girl's control, and therefore attempts to reinforce 'appropriate' behaviour were doomed to failure.

This view is supported by a move away from the behavioural approach within many schools for pupils with severe or profound learning difficulties. Assessing girls with Rett Syndrome on a skills-based checklist derived from typical development graphically illustrates their absence of typical observable behaviours. Typical development pre-supposes a child moving forward in their ability to move around their world and manipulate objects within it. Given their apraxia and physical disabilities, such an assessment not only highlights what they cannot do but also prescribes unattainable objectives on which to work next. In addition, the behaviourist approach tends to carve up learning processes into arbitrary categories, for example, separating out language work from cognitive work, and so offering discrete morsels of learning, out of context with a child's understanding.

Conductive education

Conductive education, also sometimes referred to as the Peto method, is a system devised in Hungary for teaching people with motor disorders through an intensive integrated programme combining physical and intellectual skills teaching. Specially trained conductors combine the role of therapist and teacher, taking responsibility for individual children's progress.

Aspects of conductive education were being explored with girls with Rett Syndrome, with some reported success. For example, rhythmical intention, in which motor movements are practised to rhymes and counting ('I lift my leg up, up, up – 1,2,3) seemed – to two teachers – to assist their girls in overcoming their delayed response and apraxia. Language used is kept as simple as possible, so that the pupil has a better chance of understanding it. The same language is used each time a movement, or series of movements, is performed. There is always a direct relationship between the language used and the action taken. The use of rhythm seemed to give the girls time to complete a movement, whilst the words are spoken, or during the counting. It is possible that this consistency in language, the routine and repetition are important in helping the girl organise herself and so overcome, to some extent, her delayed response and her apraxia. Group work, with a one-to-one helper, repeated over many weeks seemed to be another aspect of conductive education methods which facilitated participation by girls with Rett Syndrome.

A sensory curriculum

'A sensory curriculum is a part of a whole school curriculum or learning experience. It covers the development of the senses of taste, smell, touch (tactile experiences), vision, sound and bodily experience. It also covers the development of the integration of all these senses to form a multi-sensory (or inter-modal) approach for the child to use in learning situations.' (Longhorn 1988). Longhorn suggested that a sensory curriculum should be planned and developed alongside the whole curriculum, not seen as a whole curriculum in itself.

Stimulation and awakening of the senses may help a girl with Rett Syndrome begin to make sense of her outside world and begin to learn. A sensory approach to learning was well-established in most of the schools visited in England and Wales. Many teachers of pupils with Rett Syndrome found this approach helpful in creating meaningful learning experiences. The following is a summary of this expertise:

- A sensory curriculum requires good resourcing, particularly human resources. The girl with Rett Syndrome may not be able to benefit from sensory activities without considerable assistance. For example, she may not be able to reach out and stroke materials, but may need assistance to explore differently textured materials. Teachers reported that the pupil found it helpful if she was told what was happening, what she was experiencing, and if there was careful notice taken of her reactions.
- Girls with Rett Syndrome have difficulty in moderating their responses, which Lindberg described as 'a sensory and perceptual chaos', particularly when there are several stimuli presented together. It was suggested that activities need to be simplified, in order that she can concentrate on one thing at a time.
- Vision is the major coordinating sense, yet girls with Rett Syndrome may use their sight in an unusual way, particularly in a new setting. It

is not enough to show her something and expect her to look and to see. Staff found that she may need time to settle down in the dark room before materials are introduced singly, with time allowed for her to demonstrate a response.

- A developing awareness of sounds will give the girl with Rett Syndrome a greater awareness of herself and her environment. They have difficulty 'sorting' the sounds that they hear, so will require a quiet environment in which to work. Girls often respond well to familiar sounds, and tapes of family voices, favourite music or sounds incorporating her name were all considered useful.

- Girls with Rett Syndrome are constantly being handled throughout the day, both in their personal care and in order to be helped to learn. However, their physical limitations often prevent them from moving around, or touching and holding in order to explore. One teacher discovered that the girl she taught was very sensitive to having her hands manipulated and persistently resisted it. This teacher concentrated on tactile stimulation of the feet, and other areas of the body, in order to help the child tolerate and learn to enjoy tactile exploration.

- The sense of smell can be used to discriminate likes and dislikes, gain new information and evoke memories. The development of her sense of smell may help with a girl's feeding programme as she learns to anticipate her food before tasting, and so become more prepared. One teacher added scents to the finger paint in order to add a further dimension to art work!

- Many girls with Rett Syndrome have difficulties with chewing and swallowing, sometimes combined with dietary deficiencies and bowel problems. While some girls had very hearty appetites indeed, others would only accept a limited range of tastes. Teachers felt that working to develop a wider tolerance to different tastes could enhance the girl's life, motivate her to accept a more varied diet, and offer opportunities for her to express likes and dislikes.

- Developing the sense of bodily experience affects the girl's awareness of body movement, of legs and arms, balance and posture. Girls with Rett Syndrome often have a very limited capacity to physically explore their environment, or even their own bodies. However, many teachers felt that they should also have the opportunity to learn by 'doing things for themselves' and not always by having things done for them. They may require assistance to access typical activities, but experiences such as riding a bike, riding a horse, being pushed on a swing or swung in a blanket were all suggested as enriching for particular girls. A girl with Rett Syndrome may not be able to bounce on a trampoline unless the teacher gets on there and does it with her. One school had a Rebound Therapy room, with a floor-level trampoline so that the child could experience gentle bouncing from the comfort of her wheelchair.

- The sensory curriculum should not be taught in isolation. Many educational suppliers now offer every facility in sensory stimulation. However, rather than sit by an 'Aromatron' to experience synthetic smells in isolation, many teachers incorporated their sensory teaching throughout the curriculum. Cooking lunch may be beyond a girl with Rett Syndrome, but involving her in a carefully planned Food Technology lesson offers real-life opportunities to increase her understanding of her world through the sights, sounds, smells and tastes inherent in the process.

Intensive interaction

Intensive interaction was pioneered in Springfield School, Leavesdon and Harperbury Hospital School (Nind and Hewett 1994). This approach developed from working with the 'difficult to reach' pupils there, finding that the traditional 'skills acquisition' methods of teaching offered for these pupils only sporadic contact with a curriculum which did not allow for them. Intensive interaction acknowledges the crucial role of parents in their interactions with children in the first two years of life. The mother or caregiver is identified as the most flexible and responsive 'resource' and the infant is recognised as an active and responsive participant in his / her own development.

A repeated theme that emerges is that early interaction sequences generally begin with the infant's own spontaneous behaviour, that the mother then chimes in to support, repeat, comment upon and elaborate his responses, that she holds herself ready to let the infant resume as soon as he wishes, and that in this way she makes it possible for a dialogue-like interaction to be set in motion.

(Schaffer 1977 in Nind and Hewett 1994)

In using mother-infant interaction as a teaching tool, teachers can exploit the role of the caregiver in early interaction in a responsive and flexible way, and so facilitate learning through regulating stimulation and offering the child an opportunity to reciprocate. An important element of this approach is that learning is seen as a process, and there is not always a pre-defined outcome. Dressing and undressing, then, is not worked on so that the child becomes more independent – this would be unrealistic for many pupils – but as an opportunity to play games (peek-a-boo), tickle, talk, sing and give the child opportunities to respond. To parents, this comes naturally, and they may find the activities familiar and unremarkable, but the aim is mutual enjoyment, interest and delight in order that the pupil is recognised as an active participant with much to offer.

Some of the teachers in the schools visited were, often unconsciously, incorporating this approach in their work with girls with Rett Syndrome. It was certainly an approach witnessed in many homes.

Riach (1992) studied two girls with Rett Syndrome in order to consider educational strategies and their wider implications. Two activities, planned to develop purposeful use of hand and eyes during interactions, were described as 'not intending to test the girls' performance but . . . to facilitate anticipation, recognition and response through recognisable channels'. Rather than simply measure the number of times a girl used her hands or eyes purposefully (a behaviourist method), Riach combined the sensory curriculum with intensive interactions in order to allow the girls the opportunity to indicate choices, enjoy social interactions and communicate in whatever way was appropriate to them. Careful assessment, using a video camera and the Affective Communication Assessment (Coupe et al. 1985), enabled Riach to record in detail the girls' means of communicating interest, boredom, likes and dislikes which could then be recognised and acted on in other aspects of her life.

Facilitated communication

Facilitated communication is a controversial method of assisting people with developmental disabilities to communicate, by means of another person (a facilitator) physically assisting a client to spell out messages on a keyboard. Advocates of this system argue that it can reveal unexpected literacy in the 'seriously intellectually impaired', while critics consider the method unsubstantiated and questionable.

Given the girls' profound learning difficulties, stereotypical hand movements which increase under stress, dislike of the hands being manipulated, apraxia and delayed response it would not appear to be a valid method for girls with Rett Syndrome unless more thorough research and evaluation is undertaken.

Education for personal and social development

Personal and social development is an essential feature of human life. Personal and social development incorporates self-image, self-esteem, self-respect, decision-making, exercising choice, making good relationships, confidence and a sense of personal worth.

Her Majesty's Inspectorate (1979) described the personal and social development of pupils as 'the central purpose of education'. *The Whole Curriculum* (NCC 1990a) stated that 'the personal and social development of pupils is a major aim of education; personal and social education being the means by which this aim is achieved'.

The National Curriculum council outlined five cross-curricular themes to be included in schools' curricular provision, which were health education; careers education and guidance; education for citizenship; education for economic and industrial understanding and environmental education.

The NCC did not prescribe the nature of the 'whole' pupil who was to be developed by 'the whole curriculum', but considered that these five themes were concerned with the various 'selves' of each individual pupil:

- the bodily, or physical, self;
- the sexual self;
- the social self;
- the vocational self;
- the moral / political self;
- the self as learner;
- the self in the organisation.

(Sebba *et al.* 1993)

One might also add 'the emotional self' to this list.

It is with this 'whole self' that education for personal and social development is concerned. Girls with Rett Syndrome must be seen as having a capacity to learn, as individuals with their own personalities and preferences.

For many years, educational progress in special schools was measured in notions of remediation and 'normalisation'. The aim of many schools was to attempt to minimise and 'cure' idiosyncrasies and channel pupils towards more 'socially acceptable' behaviour. The power remained with the professionals – albeit in partnership with parents – and often perpetuated dependency in pupils with learning disabilities. For example, augmentative communication, such as signing, symbols or using a technological aid, may be confined to specific lessons on the timetable. This offers no opportunity for generalising the skills and communicating spontaneously. This was illustrated time and again when girls with Rett Syndrome were reported as only using a few formal methods of communicating in school, while their parents described a wealth of ways in which they communicated at home. Conversely, help and guidance may be offered at different levels between home and school, for example one girl was an independent eater at school and totally dependent at home.

Sadly, some schools – although, perhaps, believing that they were acting in the best interests of the girl with Rett Syndrome – were observed exercising power and control over the girls. This was illustrated in one school which tied a girl's hands to the arms of her wheelchair in order to prevent stereotypical hand movements, and in another where a senior manager of the school sat alongside a child and stated 'There's not much there'. Most schools visited, however, were attempting to allow their girls with Rett Syndrome to develop more self-esteem and autonomy. This was achieved by recognising and acting upon the signals the girls were able to give regarding their likes, dislikes and preferences, building on their interests in order to motivate them, giving them time to respond and accepting them as whole, rather than incomplete, people.

The additional curriculum

Access to the National Curriculum and an appropriate developmental curriculum does not meet all the needs of a girl with Rett Syndrome.

Equally important is the need for physiotherapy, speech and language therapy, occupational therapy, hydrotherapy and individual medical support and these form the additional curriculum for each individual pupil. Meeting the educational needs of the girls can only be effective within meeting their needs as people. Their disabilities result in varied and complex personal needs in addition to their educational needs, and these additional needs are met by a variety of professionals.

Teachers, although perhaps experienced with disabilities, are not paramedics. However, there are a wealth of other professionals from whom expertise can be sought. An holistic approach to teaching and learning will be required in order to become effective in meeting the whole needs of the girl with Rett Syndrome.

There is a danger, when different areas of need are the domain of different professionals, that each aspect of learning is fragmented and isolated from the whole curriculum. All professionals, therefore, should collaborate in order to ensure there is a consistent approach.

The Code of Practice, issued by the Secretary of State for Education following the 1993 Education Act, stated that 'Many children with special educational needs have a range of difficulties and the achievement of educational objectives is likely to be delayed without partnership between all concerned.' (2:27)

For children under the age of two, a Statement of special educational need must include:

- all available information about the child, with a clear specification of the child's special educational needs;
- a record of the views of parents and any relevant professionals. (5:6)

As the child moves into full-time education at five, the school must 'alert any relevant support or external professionals at the earliest possible stage' (5:29).

At each Annual Review of the child's statement, the Local Education Authority or the school may invite representatives from the health services or social services department to contribute to the review. These authorities are required, by section 166 (1) of the Education Act (1993) to respond to such a request either by submitting a report, or attending the Annual review meeting. (6.22) A child's changing needs must be identified within the Annual Review report, and the LEA may then amend the child's statement. (6.27)

The first Annual Review after a young person's fourteenth birthday is an important one, although it broadly follows previous annual review procedures. However, in addition to other points, the LEA must:

> ensure that other providers, such as social services, are aware of the annual review and the procedures to be followed, and must invite the social services department to attend the review so that any parallel assessments under the Disabled Persons Act (1986); the NHS and Community Care Act (1990); and the Chronically Sick and Disabled Persons Act (1970) can contribute to and draw information from the review process (6:44)

During or following this annual review, a Transition Plan is drawn up, which draws together information from a range of individuals within and beyond the school in order to plan coherently for the young person's transition to adult life. This Transition Plan must be reviewed at each subsequent annual review.

LEAs must also consult child health services and any other professionals who may have a useful contribution to make. (6:45)

The Code of Practice sets out the questions which must be addressed within the Transition Plan, and includes the questions which must be considered by all professionals involved with the child:

- How can (the professionals) develop close working relationships with colleagues in other agencies in order to ensure effective and coherent plans for the young person in transition?
- Which new professionals need to be involved in planning for transition, for example occupational psychologists; a rehabilitation medicine specialist; occupational and other therapists?
- Does the young person have any special health or welfare needs which will require planning and support from health and social services now or in the future?
- Are assessment arrangements for transition clear, relevant and shared between all agencies concerned?
- How can information best be transferred from children's to adult services to ensure a smooth transition?
- Where a young person requires a particular technological aid, do the arrangements for transition include appropriate training and arrangements for securing technological support?

And for the family:

- Will parents experience new care needs and require practical help in terms of aids, adaptations or general support during these years? (6:46)

The Code of Practice thus enshrines the principles of inter-agency collaboration in good practice, but not, unfortunately, in law. However 'all those to whom the Code applies have a statutory duty to have regard to it; they must not ignore it'. (Foreword to the Code of Practice, page ii).

A multi-disciplinary team approach, must, therefore be part of a school's culture. Parents and therapists are an integral part of the girl with Rett Syndrome's learning experience, and their full involvement can support the appropriate delivery of the curriculum.

In the study of 42 girls with Rett Syndrome, the educational priorities identified by teachers were as follows, in order of importance: (Suggested relevant professionals appear alongside, although this is not an exhaustive list).

- Communication: (speech and language therapist/music therapist);
- Mobility/motor development (physiotherapist/medical officer);
- Social skills/leisure (music therapist/social services);
- Independence/lifeskills (physiotherapist/occupational therapist);
- Cognitive skills (speech and language therapist/educational psychologist);
- Fine motor skills/hand function (occupational therapist).

The study explored the input of therapists to the education of girls with Rett Syndrome. More recent research, compiling a database for the United Kingdom Rett Syndrome Association (Lewis 1995, unpublished) collates data on the provision of services for 319 girls with Rett Syndrome in England and Wales.

The physiotherapist

The physiotherapist is concerned with movement, and can improve problems of motor co-ordination and physical disability by passive and active treatment and by the provision of personal mobility aids. From the UKRSA database, it emerges that 44 per cent of girls with Rett Syndrome can walk unaided, and of the remainder half can walk with assistance and half do not walk at all. It is also interesting to note that their level of walking ability largely remains unchanged over a period of time. 'In particular, although a small percentage of girls go off their feet with increasing age, the percentage of girls walking unaided is surprisingly constant across the age bands' (Cass 1993).

Within the initial study of 42 girls, 18 saw a physiotherapist once a week, and 11 others had access to occasional advice. One pupil (in Canada) saw her physiotherapist three times per week. The database confirms this picture, showing that 77 per cent of girls receive some level of therapy, although the exact extent in each case is unknown. It would appear that a significant percentage of girls receive no physiotherapy at all. This great need requires addressing for all.

Hydrotherapy

Hydrotherapy is, simply, physiotherapy in water. The provision of hydrotherapy, therefore, links closely with physiotherapy provision. The database indicates that around 45 per cent of girls receive hydrotherapy.

The speech and language therapist

The speech and language therapist, working within a special school, is concerned with communication in its widest sense. The therapist may set up individual programmes to develop receptive and expressive communication skills, and will also have much to offer in devising feeding programmes. The speech and language therapist may also be able to arrange independent assessment regarding the suitability of technological aids to develop communication.

Twelve girls in the initial study had weekly contact with a speech therapist, one having daily individual time. The database concurs, illustrating that 36 per cent receive speech and language therapy.

The development of communication skills in girls with Rett Syndrome was the highest priority by most teachers. Many of them, evidently, are attempting to teach this area without the support of the speech and language therapist in assessing the girl and assisting in planning appropriate work.

The occupational therapist

The occupational therapist assists in independence training, and in recreational and daily living skills. These therapists work specifically on developing hand function, and can advise and supply aids to assist a child in minimising her disability.

Eight girls (almost 20 per cent) in the initial study regularly saw an occupational therapist, an inadequate picture made worse by the database findings of 10 per cent of the 319 girls with Rett Syndrome. This discrepancy can be explained as the smaller study involved girls in America and Canada, where entitlement to therapies is enshrined in law, whereas the database contains information regarding provision in England and Wales only. As all girls suffer from impaired hand function, the absence of occupational therapy for most is inexplicable.

Where girls with Rett Syndrome had received specific work designed to improve and maintain hand function, their ability to use their hands appeared much improved. One young lady, for example, had the ability to pick up raisins from a small pot and transfer them to her mouth. Where, too, a late diagnosis had not highlighted the aspect of impaired hand function, this area had been worked on automatically and the use of hands was comparatively good. This is an area which would benefit from further study.

The music therapist

The qualified music therapist uses music in the amelioration of a broad spectrum of special needs. This is achieved both through listening to music and/or composing and improvising. Music therapy is reported to offer a means of engaging children with whom normal communication through language is difficult or impossible, a means of creating an awareness of sound, and a means of relieving tension in people with special needs.

Eight girls in the initial study received music therapy, either individually or in groups. The picture improves in the database, indicating that over 30 per cent of the girls receive music therapy. It is unclear whether or not this is provided within school, or privately at home.

Other therapies

Some girls were receiving other therapies, but the numbers were so small as to be statistically negligible. These include Riding for the Disabled, aromatherapy, reflexology, rebound therapy and cranial osteopathy.

The curriculum for girls with Rett Syndrome

Girls with Rett Syndrome in the UK were demonstrated to be working within the National Curriculum across the breadth of subjects. Certain subjects were more strongly represented in their timetable, for example, the core subjects of English, mathematics and science, the foundation subjects music and PE and the cross-curricular themes information technology and personal and social education.

The developmental curriculum for girls with Rett Syndrome was being used for some sound and/or innovative work, such as conductive education techniques, a sensory approach to the curriculum, and intensive interaction. Some of the best work was observed where schools had taken education for personal and social development as their underlying principle at the heart of their curriculum content and delivery.

Girls with Rett Syndrome have been shown to have a great need for an additional curriculum in order to meet their needs. In order to prevent fragmented learning experiences, a multi-disciplinary approach was advocated. In practice, this was seldom achieved. Many do not receive the specialist support to which they are entitled.

There is a need for further research into the value of specific therapies. In particular, there was a lack of occupational therapy for many girls, combined with some evidence of great benefits to them in maintaining and improving hand function where this therapy had been delivered.

An appropriate curriculum

The fundamental question of whether the National Curriculum is an appropriate curriculum for pupils with profound learning difficulties as yet remains unanswered. However, girls with Rett Syndrome are entitled to a broad, balanced, relevant and differentiated curriculum. This is not empty rhetoric, but sound curriculum philosophy.

Despite detailed curriculum guidance over a prolonged period of time, it is still left to schools to implement what they consider to be the whole curriculum. There remains much work to be done in interpreting the National Curriculum for girls with Rett Syndrome. Subjects which have traditionally focused on more advanced levels need to be defined appropriately at the earliest levels in order to avoid tokenism. Schools will need to address whether they can make 'handwriting' appropriate for girls with Rett Syndrome, or whether to disapply her from this attainment target. Whatever is decided at age 5 might be re-evaluated at age 15.

The practice common in many of the schools visited was to consider physiotherapy as a physical education lesson for a girl with Rett Syndrome. Whilst to some extent this is a pragmatic solution, physiotherapy does not incorporate all the physical education attainment targets. Girls will also enjoy and benefit from dance and gymnastics at an appropriate level.

Aspects of the developmental curriculum, for example, a sensory curriculum, can be helpful in giving the girl access to the National Curriculum. However, it is one possible approach. Careful timetabling will be needed in order to prevent a girl from receiving her 'whole curriculum' in the same way. For example, the dark room may be used to work on science (light/electricity); maths (perceptual skills); English (use of an illuminated writing board) and leisure (because she likes it).

While no-one could dispute the value of activities such as use of a sensory environment, it is also important to consider why it is being used – what are the planned learning experiences? If planned teaching is divided into man-made compartments (subjects) then effective learning will not be enhanced. Girls will need to explore science, learn about maths and develop their communication through activities and experiences which encompass these aspects, but which are useful and meaningful in themselves.

It is also necessary to consider the purpose of any such planned teaching and learning. What use is working on 'tasting' every week if it doesn't inform staff who are helping her eat her lunch? Careful recording and reporting will ensure that information about girls' likes, dislikes and progress is not lost, but shared and passed on to improve the quality of their lives.

Assessment

There is a need for careful, observational assessment over a period of time, in order to plan a girl's learning needs. Checklists are unlikely to provide sufficient information about her skills or correctly define possible future areas of work. Noting how she reacts in various settings, on different days and combining this with information from parents and other professionals will afford a more accurate indication of her skills and potential.

Information and communication technology

Many girls with Rett Syndrome respond well to equipment which gives a big impact for little effort, particularly if it also offers strong sensory stimulation. Switches which control light/sound equipment and music technology all motivate many girls. Information and communication technology gives the pupil a rare opportunity to communicate, to gain access to a wider curriculum and to control the environment in which she lives.

Conductive education

Aspects of conductive education have been found to be helpful for the girls to overcome some of their apraxic or delayed motor movements. Rhythmic intention is a good example which, at best, reinforces her intentions to move, may link with music to help her relax and so minimise the effort and concentration required and offers opportunities for several professionals to work together in planning to meet her special educational needs.

Intensive interaction

Recognising that the girl is an active participant and allowing her opportunities to make choices, enjoy social interactions and communicate by whatever means are available to her, would seem to offer many opportunities to promote learning in the child with Rett Syndrome.

Multi-professional collaboration

There is a great need for inter-agency collaboration in meeting the educational needs of girls with Rett Syndrome. This has been illustrated many times elsewhere. Joint planning ensures that she will enjoy a consistent approach and that her learning is not disjointed and fragmented. The Code of Practice offers one way of beginning this process, advocating collaboration between different professionals, the setting of objectives and the involvement of parents and the child herself if possible. While it is unlikely that the girl with Rett Syndrome could express all her thoughts at her annual review, people who know her well can represent her point of view from their thorough knowledge of her reactions and responses in all areas of her education.

For girls who do not receive support from other professionals – physiotherapists, occupational therapists, speech and language therapists – their annual review may be a convenient time at which to seek such involvement. If such a need is agreed then the LEA may be approached in order to consider a re-assessment of her statement of special educational needs. This should ensure that her needs are met more fully in the future.

Girls with Rett Syndrome are complete and whole people. They are not divided into parts which need to be educated, parts which need to be cared for and parts that need to be healthy. Ensuring their health, care and education requires an holistic approach and their quality of life must embody these things. Cognisance of each subject area to which she is entitled in her curriculum will, however, ensure that she receives breadth and balance rather than a narrow, prescriptive education.

Chapter 10

Specific Teaching Strategies

In the previous chapters, the factors that affect the learning of girls with Rett Syndrome have been discussed, along with the barriers that the condition presents. In this chapter, strategies are suggested that may help with her physical, social, emotional and intellectual well-being. Some of these may well be considered important for all children, and particularly so for any pupil with a profound and multiple learning difficulty. However, Rett Syndrome produces additional barriers – apraxia, hand dysfunction and delayed response, which present additional challenges when designing an appropriate educational programme.

The suggested strategies have been organised around the theoretical model referred to earlier in this book and reflect the various factors affecting girls with Rett Syndrome, the three specific difficulties, and the implications for teachers.

Initial strategies in teaching girls with Rett Syndrome

The Statement, Annual Review and Transition Plan

- For any child with special educational needs, the drawing up of the Statement, and subsequent Annual Reviews and Transition Plans, are very important both in determining school placement, and in monitoring the effectiveness of that placement. The Statement outlines the child's special educational needs, identifies an appropriate school and outlines the resources provided to meet her needs. Annual Review provides an opportunity each year to look at her progress and review her education. A Transition Plan, drawn up at the first Annual Review following the fourteenth birthday, outlines plans for post-school provision.

- Parental involvement is sought by the LEA and / or the school, as it is vital to take into account their views, observations, concerns and needs if priorities are to be addressed. All concerned should also be aware that there may be occasions when different people identify different priorities. The starting point must be the needs of the pupil, but it must also be recognised that the school's aims, available resources, staffing and time will inevitably influence decisions.
- Further details of the Statement of Special Educational Need, Annual Review and Transition Plan procedures have been outlined in a paper for parents available through the RSAUK (Lewis and Wilson 1995).

School and class placement

- Within this study, girls were observed in a variety of educational settings, from the 'most restrictive' (special classes for girls with Rett Syndrome within residential special schools) to the 'least restrictive' (day mainstream schools). The majority of girls, however, in common with other pupils with profound and multiple learning difficulties, were being educated within special schools.
- Girls have been observed, and were reported as being successfully educated, in classes from as small as 2 to a standard-size mainstream class of about 32. Good practice has been observed across the whole range of class sizes and settings, whether within an integrated place in a mainstream school, or a specialist class within a special school.
- Girls with Rett Syndrome need to feel relaxed and confident in order to concentrate. Anxiety and stress will mean that apraxia and hand movements will intensify, and responses will be poor. It is evident that sometimes the slightest bit of unexpected noise can alarm and frighten the girl, destroying her confidence and will to succeed. This is not to say that life need always be quiet. Many girls enjoy loud rock music and a lively, busy atmosphere in the classroom or learning situation. Noise that is expected by her can be dealt with and responded to.
- Work will be sometimes be most successful in a one-to-one situation in a quiet, distraction-free area. Consider making the pupil her own area, where her particular resources can be located, to become 'her place'.

- Structuring the room so as to enable choice is successful in assisting communication, for example, with tables set up for drinks, snacks, music tapes, and anything else particularly interesting to the individual or group. For pupils able to walk, a direct choice can be made by approaching the specific area of the classroom or table. Those unable to approach the area independently can make choices by using eyes and body movements. However, the nature of the group, and the special needs of the children within it, are all-important when considering structuring the environment in such a way.

- With the appropriate level of resourcing, an inclusive placement has been seen to be possible for those with profound and multiple learning difficulties. Conversely, specialist classes may be in a unique position to evaluate teaching methods and approaches most appropriate for girls with Rett Syndrome.

- There would seem to be no 'best' context in which to educate girls with Rett Syndrome. The 'how' and 'what' of education may have more to do with effective teaching and learning than the 'where'. Consistency with staff, for her to feel secure and for them to develop their intuition and techniques, will have a direct impact on her education. An appropriate curriculum which addresses all her needs will be similarly crucial. Successful and positive partnership work between the various agencies can only enhance this provision.

Staffing

- When planning to meet the needs of pupils with Rett Syndrome staffing issues are perhaps one of the most essential considerations. There not only needs to be an adequate number of staff, but they will need to be trained or experienced in working with children with such special needs, and dealing with their particular difficulties.

- The girl with Rett Syndrome will require staff who can get to know her well. This will take time, but will allow her to feel relaxed and secure and ensure that she does not have to work so hard to communicate – or give up all together. The hand movements will increase when she is under stress, and unfamiliar staff may not be aware of her delayed response and may have moved on whilst she is still gathering her resources in order to respond.

- Teachers of pupils with profound and multiple learning difficulties need to be very organised. Resources will need to be organised in such a way that all equipment needed is ready to hand immediately it is required. For each activity the teacher will need to be prepared through a planned teaching programme and planned deployment of staff. Careful planning demonstrates that every minute of the pupil's time in school is highly valued.

- Whatever the staffing ratio, consideration could be given to the allocation of some one-to-one time for the girl with Rett Syndrome. This may not be required for the whole of the school day, but for periods within it. The use of a 'keyworker' may minimise the number of people with whom she has to work.

- It is helpful if all who work with the girl have knowledge of Rett Syndrome itself. Each will have her individual physical, social, emotional and intellectual needs, and these will vary enormously.

- The particular pattern of development in Rett Syndrome, all appearing to be well for the first year or so, followed by a sudden and severe regression, is unique to this condition and may affect the girls' self-esteem and self-image in a devastating way. The major barriers to learning presented by the constant hand movements, delayed response and apraxia are specific to Rett Syndrome, and were observed in all affected girls. Staff understanding the nature of the condition can provide realisation that, maybe, it is not that she won't do something, but that she can't at this moment.

- Knowledge of the syndrome can never be knowledge of the girl herself. All who work with her must guard against labelling – seeing the girl as a collection of symptoms, or not recognising her particular individual talents because they do not fit in with the picture of Rett Syndrome.

The timetable

- There are times when girls with Rett Syndrome are more receptive to learning than others. Teachers need to capitalise on these times as much as possible, since they will not necessarily fit in with the timetable. Mood swings need to be acknowledged and accommodated as far as is practical.

- Time to adapt and respond is all-important to help overcome the barriers of delayed response and apraxia. Adequate staffing levels are critical for this. The pupil with Rett Syndrome will need time to adapt to her situation, and teachers may find it successful to use a type of 'running commentary', explaining exactly what is going on, why, and what is going to happen next.

- The girl with Rett Syndrome will pick up on patterns in her days, and learn to feel secure and confident within them. Timetables and schedules, displayed and talked through each morning and activities discussed beforehand will clue her in to the pattern of the day.

- Timetables can be illustrated by symbols, photographs or objects of reference. These could be standardised for the group, e.g. a soft towel handed around before swimming, or personalised – for example, a name card with pretty hair clips attached to indicate 'mine'. Such cues will assist the pupil to understand what comes next, and if done consistently, help her become familiar with the pattern of events and encourage her to anticipate events.

- Daytime sleep needs to be discouraged as far as is possible. Unless there is a good medical reason there is no need for sleep during the day. It may be disrupting, and prevent the establishment of a night-time sleep pattern. If the pupil does happen to 'drop off', then waking must be very gentle so as not to startle and frighten her.

A multi-professional approach

- There are many areas essential within the curriculum not immediately concerned with education. These include personal care, therapies and positioning. Every activity, however, has the potential for teaching and learning.

- Teachers will need to have access to those aids and adaptations that are appropriate for their particular pupil. Individual teaching aids and equipment may need to be designed and made to meet individual needs. Standard equipment may need adapting. Teachers need to look at the pupils' individual needs and tastes and adapt.

- Girls with Rett Syndrome often have severe physical disabilities, stereotypical hand movements which are a hallmark of the condition and communication skills which teachers identify as a major challenge. Collaborative working between teachers, physiotherapists, occupational therapists and speech and language therapists, leading to inter-agency holistic assessment and planning, must be a goal throughout the girls' education.

- It is essential that a multi-professional approach is adopted, which enables planning for the whole child. Professionals working together, each utilising and learning from the skills of others, will be of great benefit to both pupils and staff. A team of staff who professionally respect each other; regularly meet together; encourage, support and counsel each other and brain-storm new ideas provides an ideal forum for progress. In such conditions children progress, and staff teams develop expertise and confidence that can have wide-ranging benefits for the whole school.

- Liaison between teacher and therapist can be difficult, since each is working to different managers, with different agendas and budgets. Time needs to be allocated to build a working relationship, allowing each to share their professional perspective of the child's learning.

- Occupational therapy support will be invaluable in choosing aids, not only for the skills and knowledge of the therapist, but also for their knowledge of recent developments in the materials and aids available. There are many companies that produce wonderful-looking equipment, all of which is very expensive. The professional advice of an occupational therapist will sometimes help make the best choice.

Working with parents

- A positive relationship with the pupil's parents or carers will assist teachers in getting to know their pupil. It is they who know the most about how Rett Syndrome has affected their daughter. By working together, combining the professional skills and experiences of the teacher with the minute personal details that can be offered by parents, a shared base of knowledge and expertise can be established.

- Times of change in the schooling of their daughter can be difficult for parents. By allowing time to discuss concerns, school staff can work to build trust in new arrangements.

- The culture of the girl's family will need to be respected and considered if the school wishes to form a successful partnership with them. All families are different, and parents will have differing aspirations for their daughter with Rett Syndrome.

Strategies to promote physical well-being

- Teachers will require as much knowledge as possible, gleaned from a wide range of sources – parents, health professionals etc.
- Each pupil with Rett Syndrome requires as active a lifestyle as possible, including a daily exercise programme for those who cannot walk independently.
- Where possible, her walking and standing must be developed and maintained.
- There will need to be close liaison with other professionals, so that the therapists' programmes can be integrated into the daily routine.
- A sensory approach to the curriculum may be helpful in meeting the girl's needs. This includes tactile stimulation, massage, sensory/ perceptual activities involving light and sound, and any toys or equipment with a strong sensory stimulus.
- Some girls need to be encouraged to use their whole field of vision. She may need to learn to fixate on bright, shiny objects, track a moving object, master eye / object co-ordination and scan.
- She may need to develop her reactions to sound – use a quiet room to assess her favourite sounds / music etc.
- The use of rhythmic intention may be helpful. This is a technique in which actions are practised within a repetitive routine with clear cues and signals.
- Sleep during the day should be discouraged as far as possible, particularly as she gets older.
- Mealtimes will be part of the educational programme and will need careful planning in conjunction with the occupational therapist and the speech and language therapist.
- It is important to try and distract the girl when she is hyperventilating.
- Correct seating is vital to maintain physical well-being and allow good access to equipment and activities.
- The pupil should undertake the maximum activity that her physical

condition will allow: hydrotherapy, horse riding, PE and dance, for example.

- All staff will need to be aware that she may react unusually to sensory stimuli, e.g. reasonable noise may seem unbearable, or considerable pain tolerated well.
- Girls may be hypersensitive to their hands or bodies being touched or manipulated. Staff will need to allow for this.
- Girls with Rett Syndrome will remain vulnerable to falling, being unable to protect themselves. This will affect situations and staffing ratios in order to ensure she remains as safe and well as possible.
- Her physical disabilities, combined with her apraxia and delayed response, make it difficult for her to undertake activities alone. She will require considerable input from adults in the class.
- She may require protection from other children or young people who may unwittingly harm her.

Strategies to promote social well-being

- Develop awareness in all who work with her, of the varied needs of the pupil with Rett Syndrome. This will enable them to get to know her.
- Consider an appropriate peer group – a quiet / noisy group will suit individual pupils.
- Allow time for her to get to know those around her in order to establish trust and friendships.
- Provide opportunities for her to experience a broad range of social groups so that she can indicate her preferences for particular groups.
- Ensure she has opportunities both to mix with others and to be on her own – we can withdraw when things get too much, she can't.
- Closely observe her reactions to different people and build on her preferences.
- Look for evidence of her initiating or ending social contact, perhaps by strong eye contact, closing her eyes or looking away. Cue in to her social signals.
- Stability of staffing will be important to the girl with Rett Syndrome. A series of 'temporary' teachers and constantly changing staff in her class will be a cause of great stress to her as time is needed for her to

get to know people and situations. However, one would not wish to advocate the situation where she enters a class at five, to leave it at nineteen with the same few children and staff – a situation in which all her opportunities would be seriously limited.

- Change, of people, class, school or group needs to be handled gently with the girl with Rett Syndrome. Lots of encouragement and reassurance may be needed at first, before, during and after the change has taken place. Learning to cope with change is an essential part of learning for a child who will always be so dependent on others. An ability to cope with change will greatly assist the development of her self-confidence.

Strategies to promote emotional well-being

- Develop awareness in all who work with her that communication is very difficult for girls with Rett Syndrome, and a strong communication attempt, such as loud shouting or excessive rocking, indicates a strong need.
- Quiet attention, repetition and selective language on the teacher's part may bring success.
- A calm, firm approach, along with gentle, gradual coaxing may be beneficial.
- Explore the use of music and the availability of music therapy.
- Consider the use of familiar staff to enable the girl with Rett Syndrome to feel relaxed and secure.
- Develop routines, discuss the pattern of the day and prepare her for the next change of activity or location.
- Consider the use of relaxation, massage and aromatherapy.
- Give constant encouragement and support. This is especially important during the regression period and adolescence to maintain her self-esteem.
- Develop awareness in all who work with the girl with Rett Syndrome that adolescence can trigger powerful emotions which overwhelm her.
- Closely observe her hands, eyes , body movements and vocalisations – they may provide the key to an understanding of her emotional state.

- Consider using video to record her reactions and then analyse them along with others who know her well and can offer their interpretation of her emotional signals.
- Develop awareness in all who work with her that girls with Rett Syndrome are as likely as anyone else to experience events which cause them stress.
- Be aware that the way you are feeling will affect how receptive you are to her emotional signals.
- Observe her moods and search for patterns, learn to identify what makes her unhappy.
- Seek information to gain clues as to how she expresses her emotions from as many sources as possible, for example parents and carers.
- Seek opportunities to develop her sense of humour, look for what she finds funny, help her to enjoy life.

Strategies to promote intellectual development

- Learn to rely on parental and professional intuition rather than tests – if intellectual ability is unknown, lower levels of demand and expectation can result.
- Stereotypical behaviours (see chapters on apraxia, hand dysfunction and delayed response) serve to decrease her interest and involvement in the world. Anything which strongly motivates her may help to decrease these specific barriers to learning.
- Observe closely to discover her favoured methods of communication.
- Knowledge of the girl and her condition will help to develop sensitivity in her educators.
- Use observational assessment to collate 'evidence', e.g. of her memory; her comprehension of words; her curiosity.
- Set up motivating communication opportunities, e.g. room setting; available choices based on knowledge of her likes; an activity which excites her.
- Exploit the use of familiar people in familiar settings.
- Use video recordings to assess her interactive and/or formal communication, e.g. with her eyes; with her hands.
- Use total communication – objects, pictures, photos, symbols, facial

expression, gestures, signs – to aid her comprehension.

- Pictures/photos may be useful to build up anticipation and her understanding of what is coming next.
- Offer familiar routines to help her anticipate events.
- Use of visual recognition (e.g. objects, pictures or symbols) rather than recall, will assist the girl in being successful.
- Give her time to overcome her apraxia and delayed response, and presume she can't rather than won't.

Strategies to promote hand function

- When girls have systematically followed intensive hand use programmes, devised and monitored by professionals such as occupational therapists over a considerable period of time, they have developed comparatively good use of their hands.
- Encourage all who work with the student with Rett Syndrome to develop an awareness of the individual pattern and rate of her hand movements, to be aware that they can indicate her feelings, and that she may dislike them being interfered with.
- Carefully observe her particular hand movements to get to know their pattern, perhaps using a video camera. Use the hand movements she makes naturally as a basis for programme planning, for example if she taps, then provide stimulating things to tap.
- Gentle restraint of the hands may be appropriate. If necessary, consider using splints (or large bean bags over her arm) in consultation with the occupational therapist for specific activities. This is physical restraint and should be closely monitored and evaluated regularly.
- Plan activities that are motivating but not over-stimulating. Over-stimulation may lead to agitation which may, in turn, intensify hand movements.
- Be aware that lack of hand-use is a specific difficulty of Rett Syndrome, and that it will prevent her from 'performing' in many developmental tests. Respect your own professional and instinctive judgement of her abilities.
- Consider the use of computers with programs that stimulate a quick response.

- Consider the use of touch screens, pads, sound beams and switches that respond to the slightest intentional movement.
- Try using music and musical instruments to motivate her to use her hands purposefully.
- Try using water, and other sensory media, to divert attention from the hand movements.
- Continually look out for toys with an element of surprise to provide motivation and develop a sense of humour.

Strategies to minimise delayed response

- Consider individual time allocation for the pupil with Rett Syndrome.
- Build anticipation, so that the desire to participate reduces the response time.
- Encourage repetition of simple activities. Computers and other items of Information and communication technology equipment may assist where the response is immediate, yet momentary, thus encouraging repetition of an already mastered action.
- Consider using cause and effect apparatus to motivate and to encourage hand/eye co-ordination.
- Consider staff allocation. Known and liked people will help the student feel confident in that she is able to predict their reactions.
- Make staff aware that during the response time the girl must be left to concentrate. It will not be helpful for someone else to repeat a request from another part of the room and break her concentration.
- Structure the environment so as to provide minimal distraction. An area for quiet working, with as little visual and auditory stimulus as possible will help focus attention.
- Consider the timetable. A quiet, uninterrupted, short one-to-one session would be preferable to a long, interrupted one.
- Try using controlled repetition of instructions in 'burst pause' sequence. This will be particularly effective if the language used is carefully and sensitively simplified, and the repetition exact.
- Get to know the individual's response time, its variations and what she does during this time so that your expectations may be more realistic.

- It may be possible to video a session and analyse response times.
- Expect a delayed response. Be grateful if the delay is short, but expect it and adjust expectations accordingly.
- Give lots and lots of praise when she eventually does respond – continually build the pupil's self esteem.
- Get to know the differences between delayed response times and expressions of boredom.

Strategies to minimise the effects of apraxia

- Try to keep the pupil's motivation high.
- Activities need to be chosen that interest and have possibilities for further learning. This ensures that an activity will build upon that which went before and will not be too challenging at any one stage.
- Care must be taken not to present the pupil with too much at any one time and activities planned so that she will only be required to do one thing at a time.
- Environmental distractions must be limited when concentration is sought.
- Responses need to be closely observed so as not to be misinterpreted. This may take time and repetition.
- Inappropriate actions on her part need to be minimised by the manner in which equipment is presented, e.g. use of clamps on equipment to stop her swiping it away.
- Effort, whether successful or otherwise, needs to be recognised and praised.
- Give opportunities to do familiar tasks. This may minimise apraxia, since the more familiar she is with a task, the less she has to think about it.

Conclusions

The future for girls with Rett Syndrome runs alongside that of other pupils with profound and multiple learning difficulties. It is time to seize the opportunity and try to ensure that the future for pupils with profound and multiple learning difficulties is one of progress, hope and equal opportunity. For girls with Rett Syndrome particularly, education needs to move away from the medical model which continues to maintain its stronghold in such a newly diagnosed condition. This may be achieved through an increased knowledge about the condition of Rett Syndrome, an appreciation of the wide range of characteristics within a diagnosis, and through relevant educational research.

Given the small numbers of girls with whom most teachers come into contact, special classes, or schools with a number of girls with Rett Syndrome, would be well-placed to lead some of this research.

Many teachers of girls with Rett Syndrome faced challenges in meeting their special educational needs. However, some of these challenges in one context were successes in another context. The dissemination of work undertaken among teachers is vital to overcome this disparity.

A number of areas with a potential for further research have been highlighted within this study. For example: developing hand-use programmes; using a behavioural objectives approach and the use of rhythmic intention. In addition, further research into overcoming apraxia and delayed response would be of value. Any suggested methods arising from future research should be soundly appraised before recommendation to parents.

There remains insufficient literature regarding communication in girls with Rett Syndrome. Interactive methods, combining needs and preferences and social interactions may be worthy of further research. Objects of reference, pictures and symbols may also offer an appropriate area for future work. Music therapy may, too, offer an additional way forward, and research into the effectiveness of this therapy for girls with Rett Syndrome would be useful. Wide dissemination of any future research is vital if it is to be of value to the girls themselves and their teachers.

Individual teachers may wish to investigate the social, emotional, intellectual and physical factors with which their pupil with Rett Syndrome contends. Parents and families may consider appraising the whole environment – at home and at school – in which their daughter lives and works, and make alterations if necessary.

Neither medical or educational research can transform the diagnosis of Rett Syndrome, but the growing body of knowledge which research provides could, possibly, transform the lives of those who have that diagnosis.

The important thing is to focus on what the girls can do, not on what they cannot, or do not, do. It also important to understand that ability is not only that which can be measured by external achievements – ability is everything that exists within, whether it can be expressed or not. The aim must be for the girl to use her abilities better, but this aim must be defined to suit her own needs, not to meet our needs of seeing her demonstrate those abilities.

(Lindberg 1991, p.149)

Bibliography

Adelman, H.S. (1994) 'Intervening to enhance home involvement in schooling'. *Intervention in School and Clinic*. **29**(5), May 1994.

Aherne, P. and Thornber, A. (1990) *Communication for All*. London: David Fulton Publishers.

Allan, I. (1991) *Rett Syndrome. A View on Care and Management*. The National Rett Syndrome Association.

Allen, L. (1987) *Duty to review*. Centre for Studies on Integration in Education. (CSIE)

Banes, D. and Coles, C. (1995) *I.T. For All*. London: David Fulton Publishers.

Beresford, B. (1994) *Positively Parents*. London: HMSO.

British Council of Organisations of Disabled People (1995) BCODP Research. *British Organisations of Disabled People*. Annual Update.

Brown, C. (1994) From an address at *UKRSA Conference October 1994*.

Brudenell, P. (1986) *The Other Side of Profound Handicap*. Hampshire: Macmillan Education

Cass, H. (1993) *Preliminary Report – UKRSA Questionnaire*. Unpublished.

Cass, H. (1994) From an address at *UKRSA Conference October 1994*.

Coupe, J., Barton, L., Barber, M., Collins, L., Levey, D. and Murphy, D. (1985) *The Affective Communication Assessment*. Manchester: Manchester Education Committee: Melland School.

Coupe, J. and Goldbart, J. (1988) *Communication Before Speech*. London: Chapman and Hall.

Coupe, J. and Porter, J. (eds) (1986) *The Education of Children with Severe Learning Difficulties*. London: Croom Helm.

Department for Education (1993) *Education Act*. London: HMSO.

Department for Education (1994) *Code of Practice on the Identification and Assessment of Special Educational Needs*. Central Office of Information.

Department for Education (1994) *Special Educational Needs. A Guide for Parents*. London: HMSO.

Department of Education and Science (1971) *Education Act (Handicapped Children)*. London: HMSO.

Department of Education and Science (1978) *Special Educational Needs: Report of the Committee of Inquiry into The Education of Handicapped Children and Young People*. (The Warnock Report) London: HMSO.

Department of Education and Science (1979) *Aspects of Secondary Education in England: A Survey by HMI.* London: HMSO.

Department of Education and Science (1981) *Education Act 1981.* London: HMSO.

Department of Education and Science and Welsh Office. (1984b) *The Organisation and Content of Curriculum: Special Schools.* London: HMSO.

Department of Education and Science (1988) *Education Reform Act.* London: HMSO.

Department of Education and Science. (1989a) *The Curriculum from 5–16.* London: HMSO.

Department of Education and Science. (1989b) *National Curriculum From Policy to Practice.* London: HMSO.

Evans, P. and Ware, J. (1987) *'Special Care' Provision.* Windsor: NFER-Nelson.

Fagg, S., Aherne, P,. Skelton, S., and Thornber, A. (1990) *Entitlement for All In Practice.* London: David Fulton Publishers.

Field, P. (1990) 'Rett Syndrome'. *Interlink.* May 1990. Cerebral Palsy Overseas.

Hagberg, B., Aicardi, J., Dias, K., and Ramos, O. (1983) 'A progressive syndrome of autism, dementia, ataxia and loss of purposeful hand use in girls: Rett Syndrome: Report of 35 cases'. *Annals of Neurology* **14**(4).

Hanks, S.B. (1990) 'Motor disabilities in the Rett Syndrome and physical therapy strategies'. *Brain and Development* **12**(1).

Hodgkinson, N. (1987) 'Girls lost in mental "prison" '. *The Sunday Times.* 11th October 1987.

Holmes, D., Murphy, J. and Barrett, D. (1990) 'Educational services for girls with Rett Syndrome: An overview of the legal mandates and the range of services available'. *Educational and Therapeutic Intervention in Rett Syndrome.* IRSA.

Houghton, P. (1994) *Grieving, Coping and Renewing.* UKRSA.

Hunter, K. (1990) *Educational and Therapeutic Intervention in Rett Syndrome.* IRSA.

Johnson, M. (1986) The role of the school staff. In Coupe, J and Porter, J. (eds) *The Education of Children with Severe Learning Difficulties.* London: Croom Helm.

Jones, R. and Cregan, A. (1986) *Sign and Symbol Communication for Mentally Handicapped People.* Kent: Croom Helm.

Jupp, K. (1992) *Everyone Belongs.* Souvenir Press.

Kerr, A.M. (1986, revised 1988) *Rett Syndrome: Guidance for Therapists.* Paper distributed through UKRSA.

Kerr, A.M. (1987) *Criteria for Classic RS: A Word To Parents.* Paper distributed through UKRSA.

Kerr, A.M. (1994) *About Rett Syndrome.* Paper distributed through UKRSA.

Kerr, A.M. (1994b) *Review of early clinical evidence for the underlying abnormality in Rett Syndrome.* Presented to Rett Syndrome International Symposium, Portland Oregon.

Kiernan, C. (1988) In: Coupe and Goldbart, (eds) *Communication Before Speech.* London: Chapman and Hall.

Kiernan, C. Reid, B. and Goldbart, J. (1987) *Foundations of Communication and Language.* Manchester: Manchester University Press.

Kiernan, C. and Reid, B. (1987) *The Pre-Verbal Communication Schedule (PVCS).* Windsor: NFER-Nelson

Kjoerholt, K. and Salthammer, E. (1990) *Educational and Therapeutic Intervention in girls with Rett Syndrome.* IRSA.

Leeming, K., Swan, W., Coupe, J. and Mittler, P. (1970) *Teaching Language and Communication to the Mentally Handicapped.* London: Evans / Methuen Educational, London.

Lewis, J. (1995) UKRSA Database. In *UKRSA Newsletter.* Summer 1995.

Lewis, J. and Wilson, C.D. (1991) What are the educational needs of girls with Rett Syndrome? *What is Rett Syndrome?* UKRSA.

Lewis, J. and Wilson, C.D. (1995) *Girls with Rett Syndrome and their Education.* Paper distributed through UKRSA.

Lindberg, B. (1990) Understanding your child with Rett Syndrome. From *Address delivered at International Rett Syndrome Association Conference,* May 1990.

Lindberg, B. (1991) *Understanding Rett Syndrome.* Toronto: Hogrefe and Huber.

Longhorn, F. (1988) *A Sensory Curriculum for Very Special People.* London: Souvenir Press.

Longhorn, F. (1993) *Religious Education for Very Special Children.* Orca Computers Ltd.

Madden, P. (1995) 'Why parents: How parents', *British Journal of Learning Disabilities* **25**(90–93)

McClelland, R. Thomas, G., Vass, P. and Webb, J. (1995) 'Ma and pa not sold on power'. *The Times Educational Supplement.* February 24th 1995.

McConachie, H. (1986) 'Parents' contribution to the education of their Child'. In: Coupe, J. and Porter, J. *The Education of Children with Severe Learning Difficulties.* London: Croom Helm.

Milne, Y. (1990) 'Rett Syndrome', In: Hogg, J., Sebba, J. and Lambe, L. *Profound Retardation and Multiple Impairment.* London: Chapman and Hall.

Minett, P. (1994) *Child Care and Development,* 3rd edn. London: John Murray.

Mittler, P. (1988) In: Coupe, J. and Goldbart, J. *Communication Before Speech.* London: Chapman and Hall.

Moeschler, J. *et al.* (1988) 'Rett Syndrome; Natural History and Management', Pediatrics **82**, 1–9.

Murphy, J. and Barrett, D. (1990) In: *Educational and Therapeutic Intervention in Rett Syndrome.* IRSA.

Naganuma, G. and Billingsley, F. (1988) 'Effects of hand splints on stereotypic hand behaviour of three girls with Rett Syndrome', *Physical Therapy.* **68**(5).

Naidu, S. (undated) *Rett Syndrome Update.* Paper distributed by IRSA.

National Curriculum Council. (1989a) *Curriculum Guidance 2. A Curriculum for*

All. York: NCC.

National Curriculum Council. (1989b) *From Policy to Practice*. York: NCC.

National Curriculum Council. (1990a) *Curriculum Guidance 3. The Whole Curriculum*. York: NCC.

National Curriculum Council (1992) *Curriculum Guidance 9. The National Curriculum and Pupils with Severe Learning Difficulties*. York: NCC.

Nind, M. and Hewett, D. (1994) *Access to Communication*. London: David Fulton Publishers.

Nomura, Y. *et al.* (1987) 'Pathophysiology of Rett Syndrome', *Brain Development* 7, 281–9.

Ouvry, C. (1991) 'Access for pupils with profound and multiple learning difficulties'. In: Ashdown, N. *et al.* (eds) *The Curriculum Challenge*. London: Falmer Press.

Patching, B. and Watson, B. (1993) 'Living with children with an intellectual disability: Parents construct their reality'. *International Journal of Disability. Development and Education*. 40(2).

Perkovich, M. (1990) In: *Educational and Therapeutic Intervention in Rett Syndrome*. IRSA.

Petrie, P. (1990) *Adolescent Years: A Guide for Parents*. London: Michael Joseph.

Piazza, C., Anderson, C. and Fisher, W. (1993) 'Teaching self-feeding skills to patients with Rett Syndrome. *Developmental Medicine and Child Neurology*. 35, 991–996.

Piotrowski, J. (1994). 'Art for everyone's sake'. In: Harrison, M. (ed.) *Beyond the Core Curriculum*. Plymouth: Northcote House Publishers Ltd.

Pueschel, S. Bernier and Weidenmann, L. (1988) *The Special Child*. Baltimore: Paul H. Brookes.

Reid-Campion, M. (1991) *Hydrotherapy in Paediatrics*, 2nd edn. Oxford: Butterworth Heinemann.

Rett, A. (1968) Uber ein cerebral-atrophisches Syndrom bei hyperammonaenie. Monetschr. *Kinderheilkd*. **116**, 310–311

Rett, A. (1977) Cerebral atrophy associated with hyperammonaemia. *Handbook of Clinical Neurology*. 29, 305–329

Rett, A. (1985) From an address at UKRSA Conference, Coleshill, October 1985.

Rett, A. (1986) From an address at Yorkhill Hospital, Glasgow, May 1986.

Riach, I. (1992) *A Consideration of Educational Strategies for the Child with Rett Syndrome and Their Wider Implications*. (Submission to King Alfred's College, Winchester). Unpublished.

Russell, P. (1986) 'The changing scene'. In. Coupe and Porter (eds) *The Education of Children with Severe Learning Difficulties*. London: Croom Helm.

Sacks, O. (1985) *The Man Who Mistook his Wife for a Hat*. London: Pan Books.

Schaffer, H.R. (1977) From: Hewett, D. and Nind, M. 'Developing an interactive curriculum for pupils with severe and complex learning difficulties: A classroom process'. In: Smith, B. (ed.) (1987) *Interactive Approaches*. Westhill

College, Birmingham.

Sebba, J. (1994) *History for All*. London: David Fulton Publishers.

Sebba, J. (1995) *Geography for All*. London: David Fulton Publishers.

Sebba, J. Byers, R. and Rose, R. (1993) *Redefining the Whole Curriculum for Pupils with Learning Difficulties*. London: David Fulton Publishers.

Sharpe, P.A. (1992) 'Comparative effects of bilateral hand splints and an elbow orthosis on stereotypic hand movements and toy play in two children with Rett Syndrome'. *The American Journal of Occupational Therapy*. **46**(2) February 1992.

Shaw, L. (1990) *Each Belongs. Integrated Education in Canada* Centre for Studies on Integration in Education (CSIE).

Van Acker, R. (1991) 'Rett Syndrome: A review of current knowledge'. *Journal of Autism and Developmental Disorders*. **21**(4).

Vulliamy, G. and Webb, R. (eds) (1992) *Teacher Research and Special Educational Needs*. London: David Fulton Publishers.

Wadlow, J. (1992) Creating a basis for partnership with parents of pupils with profound and multiple learning difficulties In:Vulliamy, G. and Webb, R. (eds.) *Teacher Research and Special Educational Needs*. London: David Fulton Publishers.

Walters, T. (1991) 'Living with Rett Syndrome'. *Nursery World*. June 1991.

Ware, J. (1994) *Educating Children with Profound and Multiple Learning Difficulties*. London: David Fulton Publishers.

Whitehead, M. (1997) 'Down's child may become test case', *Times Educational Supplement*, Feb 21.

Williams, P. (1988) *A Glossary of Special Education*. Milton Keynes: Open University Press.

Wilson, C.D. (1992) *Characteristics of Rett Syndrome and Their Educational Implications*. Paper distributed through UKRSA.

Witt Engerstrom, I. (1990) *Rett Syndrome in Sweden*. Goteborg.

Wolfensberger, W. (1994) 'The growing threat to the lives of handicapped people in the context of modernistic values', *Disability and Society*. **9**(3).

Wolfensberger, W. (1969) In Wood, S. and Shears, B. (1986). *Teaching Children with Severe Learning Difficulties – A Radical Reappraisal*. London: Croom Helm.

Wood, S. and Shears, B. (1986) *Teaching Children with Severe Learning Difficulties – A Radical Reappraisal*. London: Croom Helm.

Index

adolescence 24, 29, 118
age-appropriate 20, 22, 30, 47
aggression 20, 28, 39
animation 28
annual review 61, 62, 80, 82, 101,
    102, 109, 110, 111
anticipation 88, 98, 120, 121
anxiety attacks 29
apraxia 11, 14, 41, 51, 53–6, 88, 89,
    94, 110, 111, 113, 114, 117, 120,
    122, 123
aromatherapy 2, 29, 30, 105, 118
art 48, 77, 81, 88, 96
attention 26, 31, 39, 47, 51, 83, 85,
    118, 121

backward chaining 15
barriers to learning 7, 12, 41, 93
behaviour modification 13, 93–4
body language 27, 28, 33, 83, 85, 89
breath holding 15

calming influences 29
cause and effect 27, 87, 121
chewing 13, 14, 53, 96
class 4, 19, 20, 21, 30, 35, 36, 51, 72,
    79, 83, 84, 93, 111–12, 118
classroom assistants 19
Code of Practice 19, 62, 82, 101–3
cognitive development 33
communication 5, 32–40, 83, 91, 98,
    103, 104, 107, 112, 115, 118, 119,
    123
    augmentative 100

comprehension 34, 119, 120
expressing emotions 27–9
expression 26, 28, 33, 36–9, 89,
    122
facial expression 27, 28, 36, 119
gesture 33, 39, 83, 120
girls with speech 27, 33, 38
pictures 27, 34, 37, 39, 40, 52, 83,
    85, 87, 91, 119, 120, 123
concentration 50, 54, 121, 122
constipation 13
curriculum 3, 5, 20, 22, 33, 57, 61, 73,
    77, 78, 80–109, 112, 114, 116
    additional 57, 81, 100–105, 106
    developmental 57, 81, 93–100,
        106, 107
    entitlement 62, 81, 105
    National 81, 82, 83–93, 99, 106,
        107

dance 38, 88, 89, 107, 117
delayed response 13, 41, 49–52, 89,
    94, 99, 110, 112, 113, 114, 117,
    119, 121–2, 123
developmental assessments 32, 34, 35,
    72
diagnosis 42, 63–5
diet 13, 96
distraction 50, 121

Education Act (1970) 9, 80
Education Reform Act (The) 61, 81
educational priorities 103
emotional development 23, 24–5, 54

emotions 23–31, 44, 118
English 83–4, 106, 107
environment 12, 30, 43, 50, 71, 87, 88, 89, 96, 108, 111, 121
epilepsy 1, 10
exploration 32, 47, 84, 96
eye contact 26, 51, 83, 117
eye gaze 83
eye/object coordination 116
eye pointing 83

facilitated communication 98
feeding programmes 13, 104
feelings 16, 23–31, 64, 65, 88, 92
fine motor skills 46, 84, 103
functional grasp 43

geography 87–8
grouping 20

hand dysfunction 41, 42–8, 119, 120
hand/eye coordination 121
hand movements 1, 11, 16, 25, 42–8, 120–21
hand wringing 1, 28, 43
health and emotions 23
hearing 10, 37
history 87
home 6, 17, 23, 59, 67, 68, 75, 76, 98, 100, 105, 123
horse riding 75, 117
hydrotherapy 10, 14, 90, 101, 104, 105
hyperventilation 26, 28, 45, 46, 51, 54

independence 19, 77, 79, 103, 104
Individual Education Plan 46
individual time 51, 104, 121
information and communication technology 91–2, 108, 121
integration 18, 62, 71
intelligence 32–40
intensive interaction 97–8, 106, 108

language 29, 32, 33, 35, 52, 94, 105, 118, 121
learning environment 50
listening 32, 38, 83, 92, 105
Local Education Authority (LEA) 68, 82, 101, 102, 111

mainstream school 18, 19, 21–2, 71, 92, 111–12
massage 29, 30, 116, 118
mathematics 84–5
media 62–3
Medical Officer 103
modern foreign language 81
mood swings 23, 28, 29, 113
motivation 15, 41, 46, 49, 55, 56, 77, 79, 89, 121, 122
multi-disciplinary teams 103, 106, 114–15
music therapy 2, 27, 30, 43, 75, 88–9, 105, 118, 123

objects 32, 35, 37, 83, 85, 94, 114, 116, 119, 120, 123
occupational therapists 11, 13, 44, 45, 103, 104–5, 115, 116, 120

parental attitudes 6, 62, 68–9, 73–7, 78
parents 9, 13, 17, 18, 20, 25, 31, 64, 65, 66, 67, 97, 108
partnership between home and school 19, 62, 67, 68, 100, 115–16
peer group 18, 21, 117
photographs 30, 33, 36, 38, 114
Physical Education 89–90
physiotherapists 11, 13, 73, 90, 103–4, 109
physiotherapy 2, 10, 53, 75, 77, 89, 100, 104, 107
pilot study 4–5
pincer grasp 43
praise 16, 31, 77, 122
profound learning difficulties 1, 13,

32, 60, 63, 83, 93, 94, 106
progress 1, 7, 24, 32, 51, 67, 69, 74, 75,
    80, 81, 94, 100, 107, 110, 115, 122
psychometric tests 32

regression 1, 11, 24–5, 27, 33, 42, 64,
    71, 113, 118
relationships 16, 30, 63, 66, 67, 72,
    99, 102
relaxation 14, 29–30, 118
Religious Education 92
repetition 12, 29, 52, 94, 118, 121,
    122
research
    aims 3
    design 4–5
    further 78, 106, 123
residential schools 18, 21, 70
Rett, Dr Andreas 1, 26, 42
rhythmic intention 12, 90, 94, 116,
    123
rocking 26, 28, 29, 37, 45, 89, 118

school 18–19
science 85–7, 107
scoliosis 10, 12
seating 11, 116
self-confidence 16, 118
self-esteem 16, 18, 49, 113, 122
sensory approach 86, 95–7, 106, 116
sensory motor stage 34
sensory perception difficulties 11
sensory stimulation 84, 91, 97, 108
sleep 13, 15, 28, 69, 116
sleep programmes 14
social contact 17, 18, 32, 35, 76, 117

social development 16, 17, 22, 99–100
social factors affecting education
    16–22
social interaction 18, 98, 108, 123
social well-being 17, 117
soft play 82
special care 4
specific disabilities 32
splints 13, 44–5, 48, 120
staff allocation 121
staffing ratios 19, 113, 117
Statement of Special Educational
    Needs 18, 61, 62, 80, 82, 101, 109,
    110–111
stereotypical hand movements 1, 12,
    42–8, 114
stress 13, 14, 24, 68, 79, 111, 112,
    117, 119
survey population 4
swallowing 12, 13, 14, 96
swimming 90

therapeutic intervention 12–13
time allocation 121
time course of Rett Syndrome 33
timetables 5, 29, 77, 82, 83, 87, 106,
    113–14, 121
Transition Plan 102, 110–11

UKRSA 2–3, 45, 103

video 5, 24, 26, 29, 72, 89, 91, 98,
    119, 120, 122
vision 11, 92, 95, 116

Warnock Report 7, 61, 80

LaVergne, TN USA
11 April 2011
223644LV00002B/5/A